The Catholic Imagination

THE CATHOLIC IMAGINATION

Proceedings from the Twenty-fourth Annual Convention
of the Fellowship of Catholic Scholars
Omaha, Nebraska
September 28–30, 2001

Kenneth D. Whitehead
Editor

ST. AUGUSTINE'S PRESS
South Bend, Indiana
2003

Manufactured in the United States of America.

1 2 3 4 5 6   09 08 07 06 05 04 03

Library of Congress Cataloging in Publication Data
Fellowship of Catholic Scholars. Convention (24th: 2001:
Omaha, Neb.)
    The Catholic imagination : proceedings from the
    Twenty-fourth Annual Convention of the Fellowship of
    Catholic Scholars, Omaha, Nebraska, September 28–30,
    2001 / Kenneth D. Whitehead, editor.
      p. cm.
    ISBN 1-58731-174-7 (pbk.)
    1. Aesthetics – Religious aspects – Catholic Church –
    Congresses. I. Whitehead, K. D. II. Title.
BX1795.A78 F45 2001
246'.088'22 – dc21   2002151731

∞ The paper used in this publication meets the minimum requirements of the American National Standard for Information Sciences
– Permanence of Paper for Printed Materials, ANSI Z39.48–1984.

Contents

Special Convention Session

Introduction

For its twenty-fourth annual convention, held in Omaha, Nebraska, on September 28–30, 2001, the Fellowship of Catholic Scholars chose the theme "The Catholic Imagination," first, for its intrinsic interest, but also in order to range a bit farther afield from our usual crop of philosophical and theological issues, supplemented by the many critical legal, moral, political, and social science issues in which Fellowship members tend to specialize. These kinds of issues have long been the staples of the Fellowship and its members, but the idea this time was to venture more seriously into the fields of literature and the arts. The Fellowship has always wished and hoped to include these pursuits and disciplines more prominently among its interests, but in fact they have not figured as prominently as we would have liked.

In the event, a program committee ably chaired by Father Peter F. Ryan, S.J., currently teaching at Mount Saint Mary's Seminary in Emmitsburg, Maryland, lined up a program of speakers and respondents which made the Omaha convention one of the more interesting and memorable gatherings of recent years. We were particularly happy to have Robert Royal, President of the Faith and Reason Institute in Washington, D.C.–fresh from the success of his book The Catholic Martyrs of the Twentieth Century–keynoting the affair with his talk on twentieth-century Catholic literature. More than a Renaissance scholar, Dr. Royal showed in the range and sympathy of his reading that he is something of a veritable Renaissance man; if we were previously tempted to complain about the lack of good Catholic writers, we can surely do so no longer once we have immersed ourselves in some of the many Catholic books and writers described by Robert Royal with such evident understanding and admiration.

Also on the literary front, Dr. C.N. Sue Abromaitis of Loyola

College in Maryland proved to be way ahead of the curve with her perceptive talk on "The Sacramental Visison of J.R.R. Tolkien" – delivered as it was in Omaha well before the recent spate of articles, books, and special issues of magazines devoted to Tolkien, not to speak of the widely praised film which came out recently, The Fellowship of the Ring.

Three really brilliant talks on beauty, sacred architecture, and music were presented, respectively, by imaginative Marquette University theologian Father Raymond T. Gawronski, S.J.; by working Arizona architect Steven J. Schloeder, who demonstrated some notable theological expertise in addition to his expected professional architectural expertise; and by policy talk-show host and music critic Robert R. Reilly, who just days after delivering his talk was named by President George W. Bush to be the new Director of the Voice of America.

These talks alone would have made the convention, and they were very ably responded to by DeSales University's Dr. Larry Chapp, currently editor of the Fellowship of Catholic Scholars Quarterly; Gonzaga University's medieval specialist Dr. Catherine Tkacz; and by noted Dominican scholar Father Basil Cole.

Barbara R. Nicolosi, a screenwriter who actually works in Hollywood, provided a stimulating change of pace, both in her talk as printed here, and in the film clips she showed at the convention; she showed that the cinema is indeed a powerful and unique art form in its own right, and deserves the serious attention of Catholics.

An extra benefit for those attending the Omaha convention–and those with this volume now in hand–was the special session held on the Holy See's new 2001 document on liturgical translation, Liturgiam Authenticam. Presenters at this special session included Helen Hull Hitchcock, editor of the Adoremus Bulletin; Father Jerry Pokorsky, of the priests' liturgical organization, Credo; and, once again–doing double duty at this convention!–Father Raymond T. Gawronski, S.J., with pertinent reflections on today's liturgy. It was, of course, a happy accident that these talks on the liturgy accorded so nicely with the overall convention theme–which among other topics included those with such relevance to the liturgy as sacred architecture and music.

Omaha was the appropriate place in which to honor with the Fellowship's annual John Cardinal Wright Award Dr. Thomas

Hilgers, M.D., whose pioneering work in reproductive medicine has largely been done there–both at Creighton University and at Dr. Hilgers' own Pope Paul VI Institute. If Pope Paul VI's encyclical Humanae Vitae represents one of the watershed Church documents of our time, as it does, then the work of Dr. Hilgers represents some equally "watershed" medical work vindicating the true (though still unpopular and controverted) vision of Pope Paul VI for Christian marriage.

Owing to a prior family obligation, Archbishop Elden F. Curtiss of Omaha was unable to be present at the Fellowship convention, but he addressed a warm letter of greetings and welcome to the participants. Bishop Fabian Bruskewitz of nearby Lincoln, Nebraska, a long-time friend of the Fellowship, was present for the event, celebrated the principal Mass for us, and preached; many participants thus had the opportunity to speak and interact with this exemplary prelate.

Coming as it did only weeks after the September 11 terrorist attacks on the World Trade Center and the Pentagon, the Omaha convention was less well attended than some past Fellowship conventions: many people were apparently not yet in the mood for travel. It was nevertheless the judgment of the Fellowship officers and board that the convention should go on as scheduled. Fortunately, all of the speakers except one scheduled respondent did make it, and so we are now proud and happy to present to a wider audience of interested Fellowship members and other readers this volume containing what by any standard are some outstanding presentations on topics of vital interest to the Church.

Chapter 1
KEYNOTE ADDRESS
Finding The Sacred in the Profane: Twentieth-Century Catholic Literature
Robert Royal

I.

Let me begin with what may seem a debatable point. Contrary to all appearances, the Catholic literature of the century just passed is both great and abundant (here, for the sake of simplicity, Catholic literature means imaginative work by Catholics). Most people – even most Catholics – do not recognize this because literature in English is predominantly Protestant or agnostic, and contemporary culture is in deep crisis – bordering on the toxic. But I believe my claim is true beyond all doubt.

In fiction, for example, we can easily name many world-class figures such as Evelyn Waugh, Graham Greene, Flannery O'Connor, and Walker Percy; in poetry, Charles Péguy, Paul Claudel, Max Jacob, David Jones, Allen Tate, Roy Campbell, Edith Sitwell, Thomas Merton, and the translator/poet Robert Fitzgerald. Several Catholics have won Nobel Prizes: poets Gabriela Mistral and Czeslaw Milosz, and fiction writers Sigrid Undset, Henry Sienkiewicz, François Mauriac, and Heinrich Böll – perhaps not as many as might be desired in a world of over one billion Catholics, but given anti-Catholicism in the larger literary world, significant all the same.

Catholic authors handle a wide range of material from the usual fictional treatments of character and plot and the spiritual life to the rich alternative world of J. R. R. Tolkien, the moral science fiction and historical novels of Robert Hugh Benson, and the metaphysical detective stories of G. K. Chesterton. And Catholic literature is not merely a thing of the past: in the United States alone, we have noteworthy novelists such as Andre Dubus, Alice McDermott, Oscar Hijuelos, and Ron Hansen; Elmore Leonard and Ralph McInerny writing detective stories; and poets such as Dana Gioia and Paul Mariani. The only genre in which Catholics seem under-represented is drama, with the possible exceptions of Claudel, Péguy, and Gabriel Marcel, unless we also want to include the young Karol Wojtyla among the playwrights.

So if nothing else, I would like to convince you of two things. Twentieth-century Catholic literature offers great cultural riches; and – something I shall return to at the end of these remarks – those riches need to be acknowledged and *taught* by Catholic institutions, especially our colleges and universities.

But an objection may arise in your minds: does modern Catholic literature really matter? In the culture in which we find ourselves, we would like artists who might help to heal and restore many things. Catholic literature has conspicuously not done so. As Walker Percy – whom I believe to be a very powerful writer, if just short of the first rank – used to lament, he might have spent his time better writing film scripts, since people do not read much anymore. And even the serious readers don't seem to be much influenced by Catholic literature. This is all certainly true, but misstates the case somewhat. Even the greatest literature cannot entirely make up for the vast work of renewal we need in theology, philosophy, and a variety of other disciplines. In *Fides et Ratio*, John Paul II specifically calls on *philosophy* to rediscover its vocation for "forming thought and culture" (#5). So there may be plenty of blame to go around for our current situation. Our discontent comes, I think, from a false image of what literature can be in our time. If we take, say, Dante as the ideal of what a Catholic writer should be – and I would be the first to argue that he is precisely that both because of his spiritual vision and literary power – we cannot help but be disappointed. Our age has no simple way to represent Catholic truth or truth of any kind. This is the modern writer's material, not his fault. As we shall see, some writers have developed quite remarkable strategies to deal with this problem. But we must be clear in our own minds if we want to get modern Catholic literature right: talents of Dante's kind are very rare. And the moment he wrote – a period blessed with theologians and philosophers like Aquinas, Bonaventure, Duns Scotus, and many others – was rare as well. So we cannot expect a writer like Dante to materialize out of a vacuum. And that is all the more reason why we need to be better readers of the kinds of Catholic literature that we do have.

It used to be that Catholic literature was seen as mostly inauthentic, sentimental, and marred by a misguided piety. Cardinal Spellman's *The Foundling* seems to have exercised a good number of Catholic and non-Catholic critics in an earlier generation. But whatever the case in the past, the opposite now seems true. Several so-called "Catholic" authors with entree into the higher culture – I am thinking here of figures such as James Carroll, Mary Gordon, and Anna Quindlen – are usually far more angry at the Church and wary of old Catholic views than most non-Catholics are. Ultimately, neither sentimentality nor anger count for very much. As Flannery O'Connor once remarked: "The Catholic novelist doesn't have to be a saint, he doesn't even have to be a Catholic; he does, unfortunately, have to be a novelist."[1] The same holds true in all the other literary genres. Great or passably good literature springs from craftsmanship and sheer talent.

During the course of the twentieth century, there was a whole series of writers – James Joyce, Jacques Maritain, Flannery O'Connor (again), Ralph McInerny, and Umberto Eco among a number of others[2] – who developed philosophical analyses of imaginative literature anchored in Aristotle and St. Thomas. All were concerned to emphasize that the artist's primary aim is good work, not sentimental education. The heart of the argument is the distinction between prudence as *recta ratio agibilium* and art as *recta ratio factibilium*. The first guides us in what we do, the second in what we make. All these thinkers, I believe, felt a need to emphasize the demands of literary form as opposed to moral uplift, or catechesis, or other perhaps desirable pursuits that, strictly speaking, had nothing to do with literature and had often contributed, as we have seen, to misguided Catholic literary work.

These labors were much needed at the time and remain valid to a point. But I think we need to be careful about this notion of making and elaborate it further. Indeed, though in artistic production as in mechanical production, we use already existing materials, it might be better to add to this idea of making the additional dimension of creating in the arts, because by rearranging those materials we occasionally do give voice to something new. Creative work is not like other kinds of work. When a carpenter sets out to make a table, he pretty much knows what he will turn out. In fact, if the result is not close to entirely predictable he may soon go out of business. An artist, by contrast, cannot – and should not – have such confidence. Creativity by its very nature has to do something we could not have anticipated, that the artist himself could not have predicted, to be worthy of our attention. The whole problem with, say, writing a satiric novel or sonnet sequence today is that we already know what to expect in both and, even when they are reasonably well made, all too often we find it. If man as made in the image of God be taken in an ampler sense than usual, we should not be surprised that what we really value in the really new work is something that, however distantly, reminds us of that primordial Word of creative origin and makes even our daily surroundings momentarily look new.

Something like what I am getting at is present in Maritain: "If creative intuition is lacking, a work can be perfectly made, and it is nothing; the artist has nothing to say." But in addition to Maritain's incisive analysis of the way creation proceeds from the human spirit, we also need something more publicly trenchant. The Platonic-Augustinian tradition brings this dimension out better and I think is best expressed by a Protestant, Dorothy L. Sayers. When Sayers was not writing the Lord Peter Wimsey detective novels or translating the *Divine Comedy* and the *Song of Roland*, she produced some very interesting reflections on literature. Taking quite literally the idea of man as Image, she puts forward a Trinitarian aesthetic that enriches the *recta ratio factibilium* argument:

> ...every work [*or act*] of creation is threefold, an earthly trinity to match the heavenly.
>
> First, [*not in time, but merely in order of enumeration*] there is the Creative Idea, passionless, timeless, beholding the whole work complete at once, the end in the beginning: and that is the image of the Father.
>
> Second, there is the Creative Energy [*or Activity*] begotten of the idea, working in time from the beginning to the end, with sweat and passion, being incarnate in the bonds of matter: and this is the image of the Word.
>
> Third, there is the Creative Power, the meaning of the work and its response in the lively soul: and this is the image of the indwelling Spirit.

And these three are one, each equally in itself the
whole work, whereof none can exist without other: and this
is the image of the Trinity.[3]

From one angle, this formulation may seem to reproduce the old
Romantic myth that the creative artist is like a god. We have seen
plenty of bad examples of that presumption in the past few centuries.
But from another angle, it ties the human artist to his origins in the
Creator. And however much, from a human perspective, the artist
may seem to be an original, his or her originality is bound to the very
order of the Creation. There are no absolutely free artists in Christian
aesthetics, except those that are bound to the truth.

So, to sum up what we have thus far, the first requirement of
good literature is that it be well made: *recta ratio factibilium*. And
the second is that the literary creation in some fashion participate in
and reflect the divine trinity and creativity. In really great work, they
go together. But if we have to choose between the two – and all
works of art fall short of perfection in both categories – I would
argue that we can tolerate a bit of poor workmanship if the vision is
original. For me, for example, Michael O'Brien's *Father Elijah*, an
apocalyptic story about the dark aspects of the human unification of
the world, has many literary flaws that we do not encounter in Robert
Hugh Benson's *Lord of the World*, which deals with basically the
same subject. But *Father Elijah*, like *Lord of the World*, is a living
and moving imaginative creation that succeeds in spite of its flaws.
A more perfect work without that degree of original vision would
likely be a lesser, merely technical achievement.

As this case suggests, we need some careful attention to understand the real achievement of the Catholic literary imagination in the
twentieth century. And I would now like to turn to some particular
works. To keep this manageable, I will look primarily at Catholic
writers in England, France, and the United States. But to repeat, the
Catholic literary universe is much wider than that. Any thinking
Catholic will want to get as full a sense as possible of what the best
Catholic creative minds produced in the past century. I will talk
about certain dimensions of several works, but a literary creation –
like the Creation itself – contains and reflects many levels of being.
And the authors we will look at here should be thought of as an invitation to the quite enjoyable pursuit of a much more ambitious, even
lifetime, study.

II.

Let us begin in England, and with Graham Greene. Like many British Catholic writers, Greene was a convert (the list includes Benson, Knox, Chesterton, Waugh, Maurice Baring, Muriel Spark, Malcolm Muggeridge, Siegfried Sassoon, and numerous others)[4] Perhaps the only cradle-Catholic writers of note in twentieth-century Britain were Belloc and Tolkien. This is not surprising, given the history of persecution and then prejudice against English Catholics. In addition, Catholicism was scorned on intellectual grounds. So despite the great differences among them, the English Catholic writers had to adopt a certain militancy towards the kind of society emerging in Britain in the twentieth century, which was both Protestant and, increasingly, simply atheist.

Greene is a good figure to study in this perspective. Literature is not sociology, and we will be picking out only one strand in Greene in looking at his stance towards British society. But it is a strong element everywhere. Greene's great novels of the middle period – *The Power and the Glory*, *The End of the Affair*, *The Heart of the Matter*, and *A Burnt-Out Case* – do more than just reflect social reality. They may very well be the most powerful presentation in the century we are speaking about of a characteristic Christian subject: the struggles of the sinner who is a Catholic. Put abstractly, that seems a truism, if one that the modern secular literary world does not give much recognition. But Greene's great power is that he can reflect the struggle accurately while making great literature.

For brevity's sake, I'll focus on *The End of the Affair*, which you may recall is the story of a writer who is having an affair with a friend's wife, circumstances that closely mirrored certain elements in Greene's own life. (A side note on sin in literature: Catholic literature, like Catholicism more generally, has to deal with some unsavory sides of life. As Oscar Wilde, a late convert himself put it: "Catholicism is for saints and sinners alone; for the respectable, Anglicanism will do.")[5] Now, we could look at the story for what it reveals about Greene's psyche – Green was always a troubled convert, especially on sexual matters, and by the end of his life was hardly Catholic at all. But it is more interesting to look at what the story actually does with the familiar topic of a love affair, which I believe is to reveal the fundamental nature of sinfulness.

Maurice Bendrix is a non-believing writer having an affair with a non-believing and promiscuous married woman, Sarah, wife of Henry Miles. But as the tale opens he's reminiscing from some time later and frames his memories thus:

> If hate is not too large a term to use in relation to any human being, I hated Henry. I hated his wife, Sarah, too. And he, I suppose, came soon after the events of that evening to hate me, as he surely at times must have hated his wife and that other, in whom in those days we were lucky enough not to believe. So this is a record of hate far more than of love....

This statement is both true and false. Bendrix and Sarah's affair was in many ways sheer animal passion, but a strange thing happened during one of their trysts. A Nazi buzz-bomb blows up the building. Sarah comes to and sees Bendrix's unmoving body under some rubble. Though she had been brought up in an unbelieving household, she kneels and prays: "Let him be alive and I *will* believe. Give him a chance. Let him have his happiness. Do this and I'll believe... I love him and I'll do anything if you'll make him alive.... I'll give him up forever, only let him be alive with a chance..." Shortly after this, we read: "Then he came in at the door, and he was alive, and I thought now the agony of being without him starts, and I wished he was safely back dead again under the door."[7]

Anyone with self-knowledge about the divided nature of even our better impulses can believe both sides of this account.

We cannot go into the details of the rest of the story here. Suffice to say that the German bomb – the Almighty sometimes needs extreme measure to get our attention – blows open a channel for grace. (Greene quotes Léon Bloy as an epigraph: "Man has places in his heart which do not yet exist, and into them enters suffering, in order that they may have existence.") Sarah made her promise; she keeps it. The affair ends, she continues on the way of conversion into the Catholic Church, and even achieves a kind of Mary-Magdalen sanctity, including healing a man of a facial scar. All this only becomes clear from the perspective of hindsight. Maurice never knows why she left him until he later reads her diaries and talks with people she came into contact with after her spontaneous moment of prayer. But the story is wonderfully rich in the way it weaves together psychological and spiritual elements, a common practice of

Greene's. That artistry is what gives the whole account believability. Rather than a straightforward, lives-of-the-saints kind of approach, Green intuited that the only way to get modern readers to believe in the possibility of grace and transformation was to show them emerging out of sin and unbelief.

In fact, even Maurice comes to believe in Sarah's God. But with unerring instinct, Greene does not have him follow her into the Church. Waugh was able to bring off such a sequel to love in *Brideshead Revisited*, but few modern artists have been successful at that direct presentation. They usually need to proceed by indirection to avoid all the roadblocks to belief that are common to contemporary culture. God exists and Maurice closes with a prayer of his own: "O God, you've done enough. You've robbed me of enough. I'm too tired and old to learn to love. Leave me alone forever."[8] Greene's Maurice believes in God all right by the end of the novel, but his reaction is Lucifer's and his wish to remain ignorant of love and to be left alone forever, if it does not change before his death, is the choice of Hell.

Greene thus not only presented a believable story of conversion but a revelation of the true meaning of much in contemporary England that wanted to be left alone. Evelyn Waugh called this new England from which many Catholics felt alienated "the motley society." The dominant forces seemed hedonistic and nihilistic; Christian influence seemed small and in retreat. Waugh savaged that world in the early comic novels and presented something of an aesthetic-religious alternative in *Brideshead Revisited*. But like Tolkien, Waugh intuited that something much larger was needed to understand struggles that had been going on in Europe for centuries. Tolkien's *Hobbit* and *Lord of the Rings* suggest how the apparently weak and comfortable and provincial beings could be drawn into a large-scale moral conflict with mythopoeic overtones. Waugh's treatment of similar material is more acid. In his trilogy *Sword of Honour*, he traces the odyssey of a feckless Catholic, Guy Crouchback, during World War II. Though there are marvelous moments of humor, irony, and genuine sentiment in this saga, Waugh sticks closer to the concrete and complex modern situation. In an often-quoted passage that may sum up Waugh's intuitions about the motives swirling around even fairly clear-cut conflicts like World War II, a Jewish woman who had been a prisoner of war tells Guy:

"Is there any place that is free from evil? It is too simple to say that only the Nazis wanted war. These Communists wanted it too. It was the only way in which they could come to power. Many of my people wanted it, to be revenged on the Germans, to hasten the creation of the national state. It seems to me there was a will to war, a death wish, everywhere. Even good men thought their private honour would be satisfied by war. They could assert their manhood by killing and being killed. They would accept hardships in recompense for having been selfish and lazy. Danger justified privilege. I knew Italians – not very many perhaps – who felt this. Were there none in England?"

"God forgive me," said Guy, "I was one of them."[9]

Perhaps a secular or non-Catholic writer in England could have written the same thing, but I doubt it. The justness of the war against Nazism would have diminished such criticism. But it is the partial outsider, the Catholic Crouchback, who recognizes that evil in his own society, indeed in his own self. It may be a mere prejudice of my own, but I associate that sort of self-knowledge with the self-examination and recognition of sinfulness that Catholicism, of all the Western faiths, has kept most alive.

III.

Some of the same currents that were passing through England were also passing through France. But France presented its Catholic writers with a much different social world. The French Revolution had, needlessly in my view, introduced a sharp division between republicans and Catholics that has still not entirely healed – indeed, the eldest daughter of the Church today often looks like the eldest ex-daughter. Intellectually, France had also modernized earlier than England, especially in the arts. Just after 1850, Baudelaire, Rimbaud, and Verlaine – all troubled Catholics – were already writing the kind of modernist poetry that did not arrive in England until T. S. Eliot's "Prufrock" (1914) and "The Waste Land" (1922). So the great Catholic writers who wrote in French found themselves in a much different world than their English counterparts.[10] Utopias and Brave New Worlds and apocalypses were written in England, I believe, because there was still enough of the old England left to make the emerging modernism notable. In France, there was no corresponding literature of the kind that says: if we go on in the same direction as these current trends suggest, look what we will be. Catholics still had a concrete social presence in France, though it was increasingly marginalized.

That shift issued in a twin stream. On the one hand, I would argue, there is a kind of continuation of the visionary modernism of the great nineteenth-century French poets, especially in Péguy and Claudel. These were two very different writers, but I find in both of them a kind of inspired utterance that does not respect the very strict forms of traditional French verse and depends instead on a kind of divine afflatus. Maritain reminds us that the old Latin term *vates* referred to both poets and seers. And many modern poets have laid claim to oracular powers. In the nature of things, this is rarely the case; and the very desire to be an inspired singer, like the desire for political power, raises doubts about the pure intentions of the claimant. But occasionally we see something that confirms the old Roman usage. In my opinion, the German Romantic poet Hölderlin is the greatest example in recent centuries. But Péguy and Claudel belong in this category too, even though the former would have liked a return to the old France in much the same way that Chesterton wanted a return to the old England, and the latter of the two, though a dazzlingly fertile creator, would probably have preferred the restoration of the French monarchy and an establishment of Catholicism. Péguy consciously took his inspiration from Bergson's *élan vital*; Claudel owed not only his vocation as a poet but his conversion to the wildest of nineteenth-century poets: Arthur Rimbaud.

A brief look at Claudel's life will help us understand his poetic achievement. Please forgive me if I go over material already familiar to many of you, but I find that quite a few people don't know much about Claudel any longer. Claudel grew up in the old France of peasant hardiness and the Catholic faith. But he was pulled away from that background during his education in Paris. He might never have been a poet or a Catholic without his reading of Rimbaud. But that wild youth was an odd literary influence on someone so obviously a man of order. Claudel's politics were staunchly conservative, virtually monarchist. He became part of the French diplomatic corps and served in the United States, China, Japan, Brazil, and other far-flung outposts. He performed his duties with the kind of conscientiousness only a French bureaucrat can muster. Those left him with only an hour a day to write, a limitation that he never resented. Posted to China in the early days of his career, he spent years reading Saint Thomas Aquinas and Aristotle, and writing his *Five Great Odes*. Given the basic thrust of his personality we might have expected him to be a formalist in his verse.

But what his imagination produced instead is something else again. Claudel saw Christianity as a dynamic energy that, first, opens us up to a larger world – especially important in the wake of the dominant materialism at the end of the nineteenth century in France. Jacques Barzun, in one of his best little books, *An Essay on French Verse*, notes the almost Biblical rhythm of Claudel's forms. But this barely begins to describe what we find when we turn to the actual verse. Claudel had an energetic confidence in God and His Creation, and there is no fear of the vast world opened up by modern science in him. Indeed, he looks on the scientific and geographical explorers as having confirmed the Christian's place in the universe:

> We have conquered the world and found that your creation is
>   complete,
> And that the imperfect has no place among your perfected works,
>   and that our imaginations cannot add
> A single term to this Number ecstatic before your Unity;
> When, long ago, Columbus and Magellan joined the two halves
>   of the globe together
> once more,
> All the monsters on the old maps vanished,
> So the heavens hold no more terrors for us; however far they
>   stretch,
> We know that your measure is there, your goodness is there.
> We look tranquilly at your stars in the sky, which are
> Like well-fed sheep and like grazing flocks,
> Numerous as the posterity of Abraham.[11]

In all the humanist celebration of this world, there is nothing to match this return of the human being to his home in the universe.

The role of the poet in this universe is not to explain but to create something that reflects and reproduces this truth. And that creation must be as dynamic and varied and breathtaking as God's

Creation. In a short passage from "The Muse Who Is Grace," one of Claudel's *Five Great Odes,* he uses Biblical, classical, and modern images to bring us face-to-face with what he means:

The vine-grower does not go unscathed into the vat –
Do you think I can tread my great vintage of words
Without the fumes going to my head?
The evening is mine! This whole great night is mine! The vast-
ness of the night like a
ballroom lit for a girl who is making her debut.
She is just beginning! There will be time to sleep another day.
Ah, I am drunk! Ah, I am given up to the god! I hear a voice with-
in me, a rhythm gathering speed, the movement of joy,
The shock of the Olympic cohort, the divinely tempered march!
What do all these men mean to me! It's not for them that I am
made, but for the transport of that sacred measure!
O the cry of the muted trumpet! O the muffled drumming on the
orgiastic barrel!
What do any of them mean to me! This rhythm alone! Whether
they follow me or not!
What do I care if they understand me or not?
Behold the unfolding of the great poetic Wing!
Why talk to me about music! Let me put on my golden sandals!
I have no need of music's paraphernalia. Do not cover your eyes.
The words that I use
Are everyday words, and yet they are not the same!

You will find no rhymes in my verse nor any trickery! These are
your own phrases. None of your phrases that I do not know
how to put to use!
These flowers are your flowers and you say that you do not recognize them.
These feet are your feet, but behold how I walk on the sea and
how I trample the waters of the sea in triumph!

This is a heady passage, and there are hundreds more in Claudel as great and greater than this. To step into his work is akin to enter-ing a flaming blast furnace of invention. Indeed, he once wrote to André Gide: "What is art but an exclamation and an acclamation, an enthusiasm and a thanksgiving, like the Canticle of the young men in the fiery furnace, like St. Francis' *Canticle of the Sun*? More than that, a kind of miming of the creative, 'poetic' Word, a repetition of the *Fiat* that made all things?"[12] I don't know if there is any greater example in the twentieth century of a poet open to the immediate divine inspiration that, he says, will teach him the *true measure of things*. The French Surrealists tried to get the subconscious to do poetic work, but the experiment largely failed. This almost reactionary Catholic was literally inspired by faith with the kind of cosmic creativity other poets could only talk about.

And the creativity was not only cosmic. In that brief hour a day, Claudel turned out collections of verse and essays, wrote several plays including – if we can call it a play – his vast *The Satin Slipper*, a dramatic work involving the discovery of the New World, a love affair in Spain, and just about everything else. (A film version appeared in 1994: it ran just under seven hours.) Claudel also wrote *L'Homme et son désir*, a libretto for a ballet with music by the man who was his secretary while he was ambassador to Brazil, the composer Darius Milhaud; and by request, *The Book of Christopher Columbus*, which was used for a series of musical and dramatic tableaux. His correspondence with several great French literary figures such as Jacques Rivière and André Gide are serious works of apologetics, as were several other volumes. The last twenty years of his life were occupied almost solely with commentaries on the Bible, a book he loved.

Sadly, little of this enormous output is in print in English; some older translations exist, generally in research libraries. Anyone who wants to take on the massive figure of Claudel today probably has to read him in the original. But make no mistake, it is well worth the effort.

Just one last passage, without comment, to give another side of him, this from the ode titled *Magnificat*:

Blessed be God, who has delivered me from idols.
You permit me to worship you only, not Isis or Osiris,
Not Justice, not Progress, nor Truth, nor Divinity, nor Humanity,
    nor the Laws of Nature, nor Art, nor Beauty,
And you have not allowed these things to exist, which are not, or
    are the Void left by your absence.
Like the savage building a canoe, then making Apollo from the
    plank left over,
So all these men of words, from their surplus of adjectives, have
    made themselves monsters without substance,

Hollower than Moloch, devourers of little children, uglier and
crueller than Moloch.
They have noise without voice, names without existence,
And the unclean spirit is there, that fills the desert spaces and all
empty things.
Lord, you have delivered me from books and Ideas, from the idols
and their priests,
And you have not permitted Israel to serve under the yoke of the
Effeminate.
I know you are not God of the dead, but God of the living.
I shall pay no homage to dolls or phantoms, not to Diana nor
Duty, not to Liberty nor the bull Apis.
And your "geniuses" and your "heroes," your great men and your
supermen, I abhor this whole race of the disfigured.
For I am not free among the dead,
I exist among things which exist, and I force them to hold me
indispensable,
And I do not desire to be superior to any of them, but to be the
man I *should be*,
To be thus just as God is perfect, to live and be so among other
actual spirits.

A very different kind of French Catholic literary figure is
François Mauriac. It is sometimes said that every French thinker
must choose to be either a Cartesian or a Pascalian. Mauriac was
deeply, consciously, and pessimistically with Pascal. His subject
matter is the French Catholic bourgeoisie, who bring him to the
verge of despair. In his several novels about Thérèse Desqueyroux,
The Woman of the Pharisees, *The Desert of Love*, and many others,
he dissects the unholy alliance of spiritual pride, material interests, and
authentic conversion that he found among the people of his youth
and after. Mauriac was very much a man of the left; like Jacques
Maritain and others, he even supported the Spanish Republicans,
who murdered Catholics by the thousands, during the Spanish Civil
War. But there is a redemptive note in his dislike of the well-off
Catholic French families. The very sins they commit – no one looks
as unflinchingly as Mauriac at greed, lust, hatred, pride, and the other
deadly sins – offer the possibility for grace to operate slowly.

Despite all the gloom and darkness, and the weak presence of
Christian hope and joy in Mauriac, a reader with his eyes open may

see that what the French novelist is doing bears a distant kinship with a great figure like Dante. Mauriac does not give us the geometric circles of sin as we find them in the *Inferno*, or the orderly terraces that "make straight what the world made crooked" in the *Purgatorio*. Modern life and thought are not suitable for that. But like Dante he reminds us that we need a great deal of time knowing sin for what it is and struggling to escape from it before we are ready for anything like a *Paradiso*.

I am going to focus on one novel, *Noeud de Vipères*, usually translated as *Viper's Tangle*, to show what I mean. It's a vision that has plenty to say to Americans who are breezily confident in their faith and prosperity. Like Greene's *End of the Affair*, it is told in retrospect from the diary of a man, Louis, who has grown rich, but who has spent his life in lonely suffering and hatred towards his family: "I have survived my hatred. For a long time, I thought that my hatred was the most alive thing in me...."[13] As in many families, Louis was of no interest to his "religious" relatives; he was rich and in control, so they paid attention to him for that, otherwise he "suffered on another planet." But Louis comes to understand his hatred – and transcend it.

Mauriac exquisitely traces out the factors that made Louis so hateful to himself and others: a mother and father who scrimped and saved to become wealthy, early obsession with making sure that he succeed himself, virtually no religious or moral framework other than that he not harm his health. In short, a combination of features quite common in the modern world. To the young Louis and his mother, the Mass appears to be a "social ritual of the rich." His mother, proud in her hard work and respectability, has no qualms about their failure to practice religion: "If people like ourselves are not saved there's no hope for anybody." In law school, as various measures to curb Church influence are debated, Louis quite naturally comes to hate religion.

When he meets a young woman of the prosperous Fondaudège family and realizes they value him as a prospective suitor, he goes to church with her:

> It cost me nothing to accompany you to eleven o'clock Mass on Sundays. For me no metaphysical ideas were attached to this ceremony. It was the form of worship of a class, to which I was proud to feel myself admitted; a kind

of religion of ancestors for the use of the upper classes, a
body of ritual lacking any significance other than social.[14]

Yet during their courtship, Louis also has true religious intuitions:

> It was one day on the road through the Lys valley. We
> had got out of the victoria. The waters murmured. I rubbed
> fennel between my hands. Night was gathering at the foot
> of the mountains, but on the summits light was still
> encamped....
>
> I had a sudden intense feeling, and almost physical cer-
> titude, that another world existed a reality of which we
> knew nothing but the shadow.[15]

Experiences such as this recur, but by the time they do, his tangled
struggle with his wife leads him deliberately to suppress them in his
memory, indeed to become militantly anti-religious in a family that
is formally committed to the faith.

And yet the most basic reason behind all this is a failure of love,
and this has little to do with resentment of social privileges or theology. Soon after their marriage, Louis' wife casually mentions to him
that she had earlier been in love with a certain Rodolphe. Nothing
happened between them, but Louis' fears stemming from his own
background well up: "How could I have thought that any girl would
fall in love with me? I am a man whom nobody can love."[16] This is
not mere jealousy, he explains, but a tragedy that "was being played
out beyond all jealousy." It involved a lack of love and a belief that
no one could ever suffer for him. The real love of that time turned
spontaneously to forty years of hatred and silence.

Though the couple had several children, the division between
them made even the children a bone of contention. The indifference
the wife had towards the husband leads him to make religious
upbringing a bone of contention. Louis is becoming a world-famous
lawyer, but at home he is regarded as a nothing. He turns to debauch-
ery and greed and suspicion that the whole world would like to trick
him. All real sentiment in him dies, owing to his growing belief that
desires are never fulfilled. Total disappointment in love turned to
near "infinite resentment." He sets his mind on forcing his wife to act
against her own faith, quoting the Gospels to her to goad her into rec-
ognizing her own attachments to comfort and lack of charity. When
a priest thanks him for his understanding and tells him he is good,

Louis says: "Question my family, my colleagues; badness is my life force."[17] At the death of one of the children, Louis sees in Isa's despair a total denial of what she claims to believe.

But his self-examination of all these factors leads to his understanding of his own heart as a viper's tangle that it is impossible to undo, "that needs to be cut loose with the slash of a knife, with the stroke of a sword. 'I am come not to bring peace but a sword.'"[18] He still resents the Christians who disfigure the Face of Christ, but senses that it is not too late to begin life over again. Much more remains to happen, but perhaps suffice it to say that this hateful figure undergoes a metamorphosis, converting near his death, "born again on the point of dying," as he puts it. His insight into the tangled family situation leads him out into simple, but deep spiritual perceptions: "We do not know what we desire. We do not love what we think we love."[19] That very desire for something beyond the sordid interests and intrigues among family members makes him aware that someone else is wanted. The desire itself is a kind of prayer. He first has to divest himself of resentments: "Forgive without knowing what you have to forgive."[20] It is rare that this sort of religious *metanoia* can be portrayed convincingly, even in the lives of the saints. His granddaughter, however, who finds his diary after his death and reflects on what it means notices that his long opposition to the Church and the familial religion harmed him and the family: "It was the misfortune of all of us that he took us for exemplary Christians." It is her judgment that "Grandfather is the only religious man I have ever known."[21]

Mauriac is able to make this believable because he allows no hint of sentimentality or Catholic partisanship to shape the story. The family is tangled in evils that lead to others and that make both good and bad characters appear different than they might otherwise be. Socially dominant Christianity itself can become an obstacle to real Christianity, not in the often facile secular sense that the pagans are more Christian than the Christians themselves. Mauriac is not stupid. He knows that where the Christian ideals are ignored, there will not be a spontaneous, natural, Rousseavian religion of the heart to replace it, but rather even worse elements of self-interest. But *Viper's Tangle* allows for the awful effects of sin in families and societies while holding out the possibility of a grace that can penetrate even the worst psychological and social shackles.

Simone Weil, writing about the same time as Mauriac, put her finger on the problem with most of the modern literature that looks at psychology and society: "Twentieth-century literature is essentially psychological, and psychology consists in describing states of the soul ... without any discrimination of value ... words like virtue nobility, honor, honesty, and generosity have become almost impossible to use or else have acquired bastard meanings."[22] Graham Greene, commenting on Mauriac, notes that modern fiction is thin because it has lost both this world as a concrete context, and the next world as a background for ultimate meaning: Mauriac, he says, never fails at capturing both.

If you read reviews of fiction in places like the *New York Review of Books* or the *New York Times Book Review* – definitely a penitential practice – you will see that what makes most modern fiction trivial is precisely this double failure. Mauriac's novels have a dark, brooding atmosphere in which Original Sin seems to have virtually eclipsed all our better impulses. But perhaps that is to be preferred to the kind of easy-going modern Christianity or secularism that assumes basic human goodness, regards evil as regrettable but understandable human error, and hardly knows why Christ had to suffer and die on the Cross to redeem the human race.

IV.

Let us turn now to Catholic literature in our own country. The Catholic writer in America has always been an outsider in several senses. First, he has been a marginal Church figure, since American Catholic intellectual life was at a pretty low level for much of this nation's history. This didn't matter very much once home-grown people of real talent began to appear and the immigrant Church established educational institutions. But it raised the question of how the Catholic writer, while remaining Catholic, would draw on American experiences and who he would write for. Many Catholic writers seem to have felt about the dominant Protestants much as Harvey Roche (the future Father Urban) did towards the staunch mid-Westerners he grew up with in J. F. Powers' *Morte D'Urban:* "If you were a Catholic boy like Harvey Roche, you felt that it was their country, handed down to them by the Pilgrims, George Washington, and others, and that they were taking a risk in letting you live in it."[23] That kind of overt anti-Catholic suspicion is much less today than fifty years ago. But in the American republic of letters, it may continue in covert, rather than overt form.

Southern Catholic writers seem to have dealt with this predicament most successfully. Perhaps it is the Catholic influence from New Orleans or Mexico, perhaps the fact that the South itself disputed the North's story line. In any case, the Catholic Southerner, as an outsider to the second or third power, simply saw things about America that almost no one else saw as clearly.

Take the case of Flannery O'Connor, one of the greatest writers of the century just past. O'Connor combines the oddness of characters in the American South with the oddness of the Christian vocation as it appears to the intellectual and literary world of the rest of America. Her specialty is the short story in which an occasional moment of grace interwoven with the outright grotesque and downright humor momentarily opens up the possibility of a different kind of existence. Anyone interested in Catholic literature ought to study her stories, letters, and essays carefully. If you do so, you may at times think she is the smartest woman who ever lived. But I will deal here with one of her novels, *The Violent Bear It Away*.

This is a story about the struggle between Francis Marion Tarwater, a young boy brought up in the southern woods to be a prophet by his grandfather, and the man first known as the Teacher, Tarwater's cousin Rayber, who has embraced the mildly liberal enlightened secularism of the education establishment. The grandfather had fled into the woods with Tarwater when he found out that the teacher was writing about him as a study in backward Christian fundamentalism:

> "I saved you to be free, your own self!" he had shouted, "and not a piece of information inside his head! If you were living with him, you'd be information right now, you'd be inside his head, and what's furthermore," he said, "you'd be going to school."[24]

In anyone else's hands, this might have turned into a crude allegory pitting Christian fundamentalism against John Dewey. In O'Connor's, I would argue, both sides have a point that she, as a Catholic, was probably better situated to see than either of the actors. O'Connor arrived at this drama by way of intuition rather than a deliberate idea, but we might say what she's after is a way to see faith and something humane in this world work themselves out – the Catholic effort to pursue faith and reason rather than a stark choice between the two as in much American culture. But it is possible, too, that this is to get things backwards: it may be that in current circumstances the clash is all that is possible. But the emphasis is on the radicalness of faith. Shadowy devils and revelations turn up in the course of the story, and it isn't always easy to tell which is which.

Tarwater has to pick his way through a human and spiritual minefield to know whether he should become a prophet or give in to the Teacher's humanism. The two square off directly over whether Tarwater will baptize Bishop, the Teacher's retarded son who "looks like the old man grown backwards to the lowest form of innocence." The Teacher believes that "the great dignity of man ... is his ability to say: I am born once and no more. What I can see and do for myself and my fellow man in this life is all of my portion and I'm content with it. It's enough to be a man."[25] But we start to see that things aren't so simple. His "terrible love"[26] for the retarded boy stopped him once from killing him. He has a side that hungers for something beyond this pat simplicity:

> Baptism is only an empty act ...If there's any way to be born again, it's a way that you accomplish yourself, an understanding about yourself that you reach after a long time, perhaps a long effort. It's nothing you get from above by spilling a little water and a few words. What you want to do is meaningless, so the easiest solution would be to do it. Right here now, with a glass of water I would permit it to get it out of your mind.

But Rayber can't get it out of his own mind and the two exert a magnetic pull on each other. Tarwater sees himself as different than Rayber in that he can do something; he can act: "My other uncle knows everything ... but that don't keep him from being a fool. He can't do nothing. All he can do is figure it out ... He can read your mind. He knows you can't be born again. I know everything he knows, only I can do something about it. I did." In the event, he drowns the child in baptizing him. "I had to prove I wasn't no prophet and I've proved it." But it was partly an accident and Tarwater only thinks he has said a final no to the prophetic vocation.[27]

He begins a pilgrimage, unable to eat for days, back to the old shack he shared with his grandfather in the woods. O'Connor writes of him: "His scorched eyes no longer looked hollow or as if they were meant only to guide him forward. They looked as if, touched with a coal like the lips of the prophet, they would never be used for ordinary sights again." Tarwater returns to the abandoned shack like Moses glimpsing the promised land. And it's there that he realizes his real response to his situation: "Aware at last of the object of his hunger, aware that it was the same as the old man's and that nothing on earth would fill him. His hunger was so great that he could have eaten all the loaves and fishes after they were multiplied."[28]

And soon after this humorous recognition he hears a voice telling him:

GO WARN THE CHILDREN OF GOD OF THE TERRIBLE SPEED OF MERCY.

"His singed eyes, black in their deep sockets, seemed already to envision the fate that awaited him but he moved steadily on, his face set toward the dark city, where the children of God lay sleeping."

No summary can adequately convey the power of the struggle in this book and its rich incarnation of much in the American context. In fact, O'Connor emphasized that the difference between fiction and abstract thought is that fiction is an incarnational reality. If you want to see that in her, however, you must read it for yourself.

O'Connor died of a degenerative disease in the early 1960s, and much has happened in American literature since. There are several writers worth attention. One fiction writer, Andre Dubus, is a worthy heir to Flannery O'Connor and writes about Louisiana, where he came from. But he also deals with the Northeast, where he taught for many years before his death in 1999. I do not have the space here to look at the wonderful stories and novels he produced, but Dubus is a name to keep in mind. There is incredible subtlety and feeling in the tales he weaves from contemporary American material and Catholic perspectives.[29]

But let me turn to the poets. For those of us familiar with American Catholicism, it is odd that there has been so little written from the immigrant or ethnic perspective. And we might also have expected that the long Catholic history of art and culture should show itself in works by Americans as well. Both things have begun

to happen. Two poets, Paul Mariani and Dana Gioia are good examples of this. I don't think it's a mere accident that both come out of
Italian-American experience; that has been a crossroads for both the
native and the larger Catholic culture.

   Paul Mariani, for example, grew up in Catholic ethnic circles in
the greater New York area. Like all recent writers, he's also benefit-
ed from American higher education. Many of his poems move
between the gritty neighborhoods that he knows well and the personal experiences of loss, death, and doubt that are common to ethnic American life as seen from a much broader culture. Some of
these contain language that is a bit too daring for an event like the
present one; others are just too intricate for easy summary. I'm just
going to read one of the psalm-like poems in his "Eastern Point
Meditations," which recount experiences at a retreat during a crisis
in the poet's marriage:

> *November 8th: Thursday evening. Nightfall*
> *Maranatha*: Sit still & learn to wait for him
> to come in his own good time. So, after the talks, after
> the Ignatian exercises, after pacing the confines
> of my cell, knowing there was a more-than-human drama
> to be witnessed in the rising of the full moon
> which would lift in bright arpeggios above Cape Ann
> at twenty-five past four, I left my room at low tide
> to walk out to the skull-shaped outcrop they call Brace Rock,
> hopskipping over the angular granite slabs, the seaweed.
> Kelp, this volcanic upthrust, until at last I scuffled up
> the seagull-guanoed rose-sepia-tinted rocks foot by foot
> to the highest point, anxious to greet my sister moon alone.
>
> But those lizard-gray chameleon clouds, which till now
> I had not distinguished from the sea, stretched east
> and down to the horizon, so that the moment I had waited for
> in the pop-Romantic Bierstadt theater of my mind
> swept past without event. Once more I was made aware
> the waves were pounding still against the rocks below,
> bleeding with the salt-comingling darkness of the air.
> Behind me, to the west, I caught lights in the retreat house
> coming on, one by one. *Go back*, the waters
> whispered, gnashing, *or be cut off from the mainland*

and the others. Go back. I understood then, groping
for a foothold down the dark-encrusted rocks,
That I would have to wait until the dark got even darker
before I would begin to see the light.
Not the *schola intellecta,* Fr. Drury says. It is
an issue rather of the *schola affecta.* That is,
it is not a "doctrine" we are after but a human being,
the schooling of the heart. Then he pointed to the bloodless
body on the cross. *This is your example of kenosis,
the emptying of yourself to fill up others.*

The dark paradoxes pound against the temples of my skull.
In chapel, in darkness now, as one more shadow bent among
the shadows, I glimpse the flicker of the sanctuary lamp
as it sets the shadows dancing on the wall, my own among them,
and suddenly I am happy. For the first time in months I have
finally come to rest. Out the crazed and frosted window panes
I catch the moon rising there at last. She rises clear above
her ashes, gold gathering against the pulsing velvet black.

We hear echoes of Dante, John of the Cross, Hopkins, and more
in this otherwise quite American fluidity of speech. That colloquial
ease is characteristic of all Mariani's work, even when he is dealing
with difficult political, personal, and philosophical subjects. He is
one of the Catholic masters of a distinctive American idiom.

Quite different is the work of Dana Gioia, who for many years
was a businessman until he retired to devote himself entirely to poetry. Gioia has written or edited fifteen volumes of poetry, criticism,
and translations, including an opera libretto. But quantity alone cannot begin to measure Gioia's work. He is one of the leaders of a poetic movement known as the New Formalism. These poets take advan-
tage of the fact that nearly every writer of poetry today thinks free
verse is the only form that corresponds to modern reality. The New
Formalists, therefore, have much aesthetic room all to themselves in
the old meters and stanzas, the kind of freedom that the rediscovery
of melody has given to certain contemporary composers, and representation to painters. Though they are often dismissed by a suspicious literary orthodoxy as mere traditionalists, the New Formalists
should be more properly thought of as presenting contemporary
material in attractive and accessible forms.

Gioia has written brilliantly about the movement in a much celebrated article, "Can Poetry Matter?" later included in a book of
essays with the same name.[30] An odd question, perhaps, but one that
needs to be asked in an age that has almost entirely divorced itself
from serious literature. W. H. Auden once observed that "Poetry
makes nothing happen," i.e., it has no practical function. But rhyth-
mic speech and metaphor are the lowest rung on the transcendent
ladder that leads us into a larger world. Primitive societies directly
understand that truth, and more sophisticated ones in the past
retained a similar sense. Beauty, one of the three transcendentals, is
a common reference point for many cultures. Gioia's essay laments
that good poetry has unnecessarily lost its former public presence.
He traces the loss to the fact that most modern poets have retreated
to universities. The problem is not so much that poets now have
steady incomes teaching creative writing, as that they write not for a
general public, but largely for each other.

Gioia seems to keep a larger, cultivated audience constantly in
mind in his own work. For instance, "Interrogations at Noon," the
poem that lends its title to Gioia's latest collection,[31] neatly captures
a familiar experience. It recounts how the poet often hears a whis-
pering voice in his head scornfully wondering "what grim mistake"
thwarted "the better man I might have been." The last two stanzas
show simple mastery in the way they perfectly fit together matter and
form:

"Who is the person you pretend to be?"
He asks, "The failed saint, the simpering bore,
The pale connoisseur of spent desire,
The half-hearted hermit eyeing the door?

"You cultivate confusion like a rose
In watery lies too weak to be untrue
And play the minor figures in the pageant,
Extravagant and empty, that is you."

A good bit of this volume beautifully traces out regrets, painful
memories, losses to death and time, unrealized possibilities. Gioia
writes of these in a common but elevated language, at times tinged
with religious images. In "The Litany," for example, everything that
we lose or fail at remains somehow still potential:

This is a prayer, inchoate and unfinished,
for you, my love, my loss, my lesion,
a rosary of words to count out time's
illusions, all the minutes, hours, days
the calendar compounds as if the past
existed somewhere – like an inheritance
still waiting to be claimed.

Most of the time, however, Gioia is not explicitly Catholic, and
does not need to be since his whole sensibility is steeped in the faith,
even when he is questioning or busy with seemingly secular matters.

In one poem, he forcefully satirizes a literary critic by comparing
him to a haughty, self-important archbishop. Another wittily lam-
bastes the brand-name-driven lives of the rich and fashionable, but
ends with an unusual twist:

But tonight I hope they prosper.
Are they shallow? I don't care.
Jealousy is all too common,
Style and beauty much too rare.

Not a politically correct sentiment, perhaps, or a prophetic stance,
but an honest record of a common enough mood.

Gioia is also a gifted translator. His version of the ancient Roman
Seneca's *Hercules Furens*, with its accompanying essay, provides
one of the most lively introductions to a now neglected author.[32]
(Before the current cultural decline, Seneca inspired Shakespeare
and many other early modern dramatists.) Gioia, as his name suggests, is of Italian-American background and has not neglected the
poets of the old country. *Poems from Italy*, a handsome anthology he
edited with William Jay Smith, collects beautiful translations by various hands of figures from the time of Saint Francis of Assisi and
Dante down to our own day. And Gioia himself has tackled the
Motetti of the modern Italian poet and Nobel laureate Eugenio
Montale.

His recent opera libretto, *Nosferatu*, is based on the 1922 silent
film by F. W. Murnau, but it does not simply fall into the campy or
sexual/violent mode common to recent treatments of the vampire
theme. Instead, he makes the story primarily into a shadow play of
dark and light in which the vampire, for all the threats he represents,

would almost seem to have a spiritual function. "Nosferatu's Nocturne" concludes:

> I am the hunger that you have denied
> The ache of desire piercing your side
> I am the sin you have never confessed,
> The forbidden hand caressing your breast.

> You've heard me inside you speak in your dreams,
> Sigh in the ocean, whisper in streams.
> I am the future you crave and fear.
> You know what I bring. Now I am here.

In the essay on libretto writing that follows the text, Gioia defines the modest but essential role of the librettist: he has to produce words simple enough to be understood, even if they are not all heard, and powerful enough to inspire the composer. He has succeeded beautifully at that task.

At a recent reading of his work in Washington, Gioia mentioned Catholicism a few times. Asked later if it was prudent to do so in literary circles, he replied that it was his modest way of witnessing. When he does so at universities or other high-culture venues, often someone comes up to him later, not necessarily even a Catholic, but a Christian who feels isolated and denigrated because of the faith, and thanks him for making it clear that it is possible to be a committed believer and a serious cultural figure. Dana Gioia is both of those things. His powers – literary and intellectual – are at their height and promise even greater things to come

V.

I could go on, about many other figures, but I will end here with the hope this rapid tour of the horizon has convinced you that there is much to be discovered in twentieth-century Catholic literature. So in conclusion, I want to make a couple of proposals. My institute just finished the first year of a project on teaching religion at American colleges and universities. By teaching religion, we meant not only the formal study of theology and religious history, but the return of religious perspectives to disciplines such as history, political science, literature, and the arts. I believe that all the figures I have mentioned – and many more I could not – are among the greatest literary figures of the century just past. There is a temptation in a gathering such as the present one to overrate Catholic authors, but I am talking about people who hold their own in secular literary studies. Until the post-Vatican II tidal wave hit the universities, Catholic authors used to be given special attention in Catholic colleges and universities. Greene, Waugh, O'Connor probably still are studied, but it is doubtful whether the Catholic dimension of their gifts and works receives the right kind of attention. So far as I can judge, French departments have lost hold on the great Catholic authors of the first half of the twentieth century; and there is simply nothing French of comparable in greatness to them in the intervening period. It is often said that Catholic institutions of higher learning before 1960 operated in an intellectual ghetto. I leave that question to people who know more about it than I do. But it is clear to me that Catholic colleges and universities put themselves in another kind of ghetto if they complain about the lack of Catholic culture and neglect the undeniable Catholic riches that even the secular institutions can see.

Catholic institutions currently talk a great deal about their unique mission. Here is one part of the mission *ad intra* and *ad extra* that is both enjoyable and quite solid intellectually. We need to *teach* these great figures again if we want to know who we have been and, more importantly, who, at our best, we are. I once taught a course on Great Catholic Literature and I think I can say that there are plenty of students who would understand, if we made the effort to teach them. I also know personally a substantial group of people who have quietly become experts on modern Catholic literature without anyone paying them to do so or without any immediate aim in view other than love of good writing. Some of these people are already teaching at universities. But there is no substitute in personal study for the serious and substantial institutional effort to do justice to a wonderful achievement. Many institutions are represented here tonight. I urge you all to make an effort to see that, at the very least, Catholic institutions give appropriate attention to Catholic literature. We have the works; all we need is the will.

Thank you

Robert Royal is president of the Faith & Reason Institute in Washington, D.C. His books include *1492 and All That: Political Manipulations of History; Reinventing the American People: Unity and Diversity Today; The Virgin and the Dynamo: The Use and Abuse of Religion in the Environmental Debate; Dante Alighieri* (in the Spiritual Legacy series); and, most recently, *The Catholic Martyrs of the Twentieth Century: A Comprehensive Global History.*

Dr. Royal has a B.A. and M.A. from Brown University and a Ph.D. in Comparative Literature from the Catholic University of America. He has taught at Brown University, Rhode Island College, and the Catholic University of America. He writes a regular column for *Crisis* magazine, and his articles have also appeared in other publications and scholarly journals, including *First Things, Communio, The Wilson Quarterly, the Catholic Historical Review, The Washington Post, The Wall Street Journal,* and others. He writes and lectures frequently on questions of ethics, culture, religion, and politics, and has also appeared on radio and television programs around the country speaking on these same subjects.

Notes

1   Flannery O'Connor, "Catholic Novelists and Their Readers," in *Mystery and Manners: Occasional Prose*, selected and edited by Sally and Robert Fitzgerald, (New York: Farrar, Straus & Giroux, 1969), 172.

2   On this point see James Joyce, *A Portrait of the Artist as a Young Man,* (New York: Viking, 1968), 201–216; Jacques Maritain, *Art and Scholasticism and the Frontiers of Poetry*, (Notre Dame: University of Notre Dame Press, 1962), and *Creative Intuition in Art and Poetry*, (Princeton: Princeton University Press, 1953). O'Connor's contributions to this line of thought are found in her *Mystery and Manners* (Farrar, Straus & Giroux, 1969) and in *The Habit of Being: Letters of Flannery O'Connor*, selected and edited by Sally Fitzgerald, (New York: Vintage, 1979), *passim*. Additional material relevant to this question appears in the O'Connor volume in the Library of America; in Ralph McInerny, *Art and Prudence*, (Notre Dame: University of Notre Dame Press, 1988); and in Umberto Eco, *Art and Beauty in the Middle Ages*, (New Haven: Yale, 1986).

3   The concluding speech of St. Michael in Sayers' play *The Zeal of Thy House*, reprinted in her *The Mind of the Maker*, (San Francisco: Harper and Row, 1979), Chapter 3.

4   For a wonderfully rich survey of these figures, Joseph Pearce, *Literary Converts: Spiritual Inspiration in an Age of Unbelief*, (San Francisco: Ignatius, 1999).

5   Pearce, *op. cit.*, 5.

6   Graham Greene, *The End of the Affair*, (New York: Bantam, 1951), 1.

7   *Ibid.*, 79.

8   *Ibid.*, 169.

9   Evelyn Waugh, *The End of the Battle*, (Boston: Little Brown, & Co., 1961), 305.

10 Maritain notes something similar to what I mean in remarking that it is easier to find examples of the kind of creative intuition he saw in modern poetry in French writers: "English poetry has developed in a more continuous way, and has not been driven in modern times to such a need for metamorphosis, nor led by self-awareness to so revealing a convulsion" (*Creative Intuition in Art and Poetry*, 256).

11 All quotations from Claudel's *Five Great Odes* use the translation by Edward Lucie-Smith (Chester Springs, PA: Dufour Editions, 1970) with occasional revisions by the present writer.

12 *Correspondance 1899–1926 Paul Claudel et André Gide*, (Paris: Gallimard, 1949), 52.

13 *Viper's Tangle,* translated by Warren B. Wells, (New York: Image, 1957), 11.

14 *Ibid.*, 31.

15 *Ibid.*, 34.

16 *Ibid.*, 44.

17 *Ibid.*, 76.

18 *Ibid.*, 104.

19 *Ibid.*, 167.

20 *Ibid.*, 172.

21 *Ibid.*, 194.

22 Cited in Simone Pétrement, *Simone Weil: A Life*, Translated by Raymond Rosenthal, (New York: Pantheon, 1976), 407.

23 J. F. Powers, *Morte D'Urban*, (New York: Washington Square Press, 1990), 66.

24 Flannery O'Connor, *Collected Works*, (New York: Library of America, 1988), 339.

25 *Ibid.*, 437.

26 *Ibid.*, 442.

27 *Ibid.*, 458.

28 *Ibid.*, 478..

29 Some people think Dubus is too embroiled in popular decadence to offer a counterweight to current culture. But his constant devotion to the Eucharist as a kind of anchor in a stormy sea seems to me to suggest something quite different about the admittedly troubling modern lives he chronicles.

30 St. Paul, MN: Graywolf Press, 1992.

31 St. Paul, MN: Gray Wolf Press, 2001.

32 In *Senece: The Tragedies*, Volume II, edited by David Slavitt (Baltimore: Johns Hopkins University Press, 1995).

Chapter 2
The Beauty of the Cross:
The Theological Aesthetics of
Hans Urs Von Balthasar
Rev. Raymond T. Gawronski, S.J.

Introduction

There is an old joke sophisticates like to tell about the pious religious praying at an altar at the National Shrine of the Immaculate Conception. Our Lady appears to him and says: "I want you to build me a beautiful church." "Where?" the stunned monk asks. And Our Lady answers "here."

A "beautiful church." A thing, a place of beauty. I would like in this talk to explore some dimensions of the question of the role of beauty in the knowledge of God. To do so, I would like to begin by exploring beauty in religious perception in general, in mystical traditions in particular, and then move into some of the thought of Hans Urs von Balthasar on the subject.

The Dangerous Pull of Beauty

The sophisticates who make that joke may not be exactly Schleiermacher's "cultured despisers" of religion, but they sometimes do seem to despise religion's humbler practitioners, in the name of aesthetics. Such aesthetes have given beauty a bad name among those who take truth and goodness seriously as well.

This is not entirely without good reason. The beautiful is indeed dangerous territory. English theologian John Saward points out that the devil does not so much pose as truth or goodness, but rather prefers to mislead souls with a false beauty.[1] St. Ignatius, echoing St. Paul, speaks of Satan masquerading as an "angel of light." We can be easily blinded by false lights; we can be seduced by sweetness; our eyes naturally respond to light; and any image which presents itself can readily imprint itself deeply upon our souls. It might be better not to look.

As I prepared this talk, I was in the high desert of Colorado, with views of a hundred miles, and a 14,000 foot mountain outside my window. It was impossible not to be moved by the natural beauty around me. Perhaps I am drawn to natural beauty as a child of northern peoples, lingering late in our forest-dwelling paganism, who have so readily found God in nature. In the words of the beautiful Swedish hymn we sing: "Oh Lord, My God, when I in awesome wonder, consider all the works thy hands have made." In spite of the best efforts of a bulldozing culture and of a certain school of church architecture in this world, we are surrounded by beauty. Children readily see it: their stance in the face of the splendor revealed in things is called "wonder." At the child's level, beyond any specific form, there is perhaps wonder that anything should be at all – that is, simple wonder at *being*, and being in such lavish profusion.

We are in fact so surrounded by attractive forms that we can become glutted, satiated: we can have too much of this good thing, and seek refuge from the lush jungle of imaged being in the starker regions of silence and emptiness.

Beauty and Religious Traditions

For many, beauty is the most powerful draw in religion. However, in general, highly developed mystical paths eschew form, image, and word, which are seen as suited for lower stages of the spiritual path, but not for the higher. Yet even a tradition as based on the *via negativa*, the apophatic way, as Buddhism, still reflects the power of the beautiful. The sublime aesthetic of Buddhist art and iconography flies in the face of its doctrine that one should let die any pull of *eros* because *eros* only draws one into more illusion. And so Zen, in its antinomian spirit, chants: "Form is emptiness, emptiness is form," and teaches: "if you meet the Buddha, kill the Buddha" – and so the enlightened monk burns the splendid Buddha statue. Because he has seen beyond – and before (or been seen by the beyond and the before?). Still, beauty seems unavoidable where some contact with transcendent reality occurs – witness the whole Zen aesthetic.

The Buddhist flight from form is rooted in the Hindu tradition, perhaps the richest of the natural wisdom traditions, where, it would seem, every possibility of human religious experience is catalogued and fit into a coherent architectonic. *Nirguna Brahman* and *Saguna Brahman*[2] – ultimate reality without form, and with form. The pundits go on: ultimate reality is beyond, so far beyond our dualities. However, the paths are varied, and providentially given to suit various spiritual temperaments. For those who need image, there is the "revelation" of ultimate reality in form – further developed in the tradition of personal worship, of *bhakti*. For others, the ultimate can be approached without images. I confess that, among the advocates of this understanding, I have always sensed an unspoken preference for the imageless path as being higher, nearer the truth.

Attempting to mediate these traditions, the late Jesuit Anthony De Mello, in his bestseller *Sadhana: A Way to God,* asks: "What do I gaze into when I gaze silently at God? An imageless, formless reality."[3] In so saying, he echoes what seems to be a general consensus that what you find when you reach the heart of God is an imageless, formless reality. In fairness to de Mello, he seems to be arguing for a purification of our images and concepts. Yet, again, the reader has a sneaking suspicion that ultimate reality is "imageless and formless" not just to our eyes, which can distort the higher images and forms, but in itself – notice the gender! – as well.

The West and Von Balthasar

Turning West, especially in the Semitic traditions, attuned more to hearing than seeing, the category of "word" corresponds to the category of "image" or "form." Let us call the way of image "cataphatic," the way without image, "apophatic."

The pull – and the tension – between the apophatic and cataphatic ways has been great within Christianity. Witness the tremendous importance and power of both the icon and the liturgy in the Eastern tradition, balanced – if not countered – by a powerful apophatic spirituality, and centuries of struggle over the role of images – of icons – in Christian knowledge and worship of God.

And so a question emerges: what is the role of form in the knowledge of God for the Christian? In a related vein, what is the role of beauty in coming to know God?

There is one Catholic theologian who, perhaps above all others, has grappled with these issues in recent times. Schooled largely in the theology of the Greek Fathers, he was much aware of the apophatic tradition within Christianity. Yet he was a lifelong son of St. Ignatius, spiritually formed in a tradition which, one might say, is radically cataphatic.[4] Committed to a re-integration of the mystical and dogmatic aspects of the faith, he was formed in schools, some of which celebrated the divine darkness, while others contemplated the revealed form.

Gifted musically, and steeped in literature, Hans Urs von Balthasar chose beauty as his entry into theology. He writes:

> Beauty is the word that shall be our first. Beauty is the last thing which the thinking intellect dares to approach, since only it dances as an uncontained splendor around the double constellation of the true and the good and their inseparable relation to one another...No longer loved or fostered by religion, beauty is lifted from its face as a mask, and its absence exposes features on that face which threaten to become incomprehensible to man...We can be sure that whoever sneers at her name as if she were the ornament of a bourgeois past – whether he admits it or not – can no longer pray and soon will no longer be able to love.[5]

Thus, Hans Urs von Balthasar became the man chiefly identified with contemporary "theological aesthetics."

For those of you not familiar with his vast work – over 100 volumes – his main opus is a trilogy in which each of three main divisions is comprised of a number of volumes, fifteen in all. Focusing on glory, drama, and logic, they correspond to the three transcendentals, the beautiful, the good, and the true – and that in ascending order. But although this is the layout of his trilogy, it might be saying a bit much to insist that truth, philosophically and abstractly conceived, were the guiding light of Balthasar's theological opus. Rather, it is the aesthetic which is the entry point, and which is perhaps most striking in his opus.

The first part, *Herrlichkeit,* or *The Glory of the Lord,* serves as the prime source of our investigation. There is an introductory volume, which really is central to his entire corpus, for it lays out his basic program: one might say it lays out his epistemology and the foundations of his theological aesthetic. There follow two volumes of illustrative essays on both clerical and lay theological figures exploring what Balthasar calls their "theological styles" – among others, we find Dante, St. John of the Cross, Pascal, Soloviev, Peguy, and Gerard Manley Hopkins treated extensively here. Then there are two volumes on the realm of metaphysics[6] in this question of beauty – both in the pre-Christian and Christian dispensations. Finally, two volumes on theology itself, both in the old and new covenants, find their focus on the tradition of "glory." Rather than attempt even a simple walk through these seven thick volumes, I would like to explore some issues around Balthasar's theological aesthetics and then circle in on our main image, that of the Crucified Glory.

Balthasar and the Image

For Balthasar, everything came down to the question: Is there a God? And then: Has He said anything of Himself? That is, is there anyone there? That is the crucial seed. A someone, beyond the increasingly ethereal – and depersonalized – notion we get when we use a phrase like "ultimate reality." Natural human mystical ascent always ends up in the apophatic mode, the *via negativa*, which denies all created reality and tries to go beyond, beyond, beyond. But if we are Christians, we end up, as Augustine did, with the infant Jesus, the humble Christ.[7] If God has spoken of Himself, then how? We are naturally oriented to that which is not God[8] – our senses turn us outwards – and so we naturally need to "convert" – to turn from all that is material, and formed, in order to encounter the unseen and unseeable God. Yet God has chosen to make Himself known. He wants to speak to us and to be seen by us; and so God has created a world precisely in which He can express Himself, and that in images.

But to get from our world to Him then presents a great dilemma to natural man, for there seems to be an unbridgeable chasm. For Judaism and Islam, mystical paths must offer ways to bridge this chasm created by the radical rejection of any notion of incarnation. Bridges are thrown from the human side in their mystical systems. For the Christian who believes God has made Himself known in form, this gulf is yet filled from our side by the projections of our human imaginations, in which the images must be purified – and they are purified, as C.S. Lewis would point out, by passing through death into resurrection.

Balthasar favors the Johannine tradition, a mystical path which yet insists on the Incarnation, on the "*Verbum Caro Factum Est*" of the Gospel; a tradition of the tactile verses at the beginning of the First Letter of John, and which, in the book of Revelation, sees

Heaven only through the wealth of images which are revealed.

Put differently, God is light. But we cannot see light, unless it strikes an object; we cannot see light itself, except through a prism. For us to become aware of light as it is in itself requires an intuition – an ecstasy – which is beyond our senses, perhaps beyond our spiritual sense itself. But God has chosen to bridge this gap, and to reveal Himself to us in form. And to reveal Himself fully. That is, His universe is not only bathed in light: it exists so that we might see His light and, following the First Principle and Foundation of St. Ignatius, praise, reverence, and serve Him – *ad maiorem Dei gloriam.*

Who we believe God to be will determine how we should approach God.

And so how we pray will be determined by what we believe. Any use of images and words in prayer is essentially determined by our understanding of the one to whom we are turning our attention. Again, there seems to be an almost universal assumption, that we are progressively stripped of form, the higher we ascend toward God who Himself transcends all our notions of form – and perhaps any form beyond our notions.

Is God Formless?

But is God Himself ultimately formless? Or some third, transcending our ideas of form and formlessness? Surely, not just a void – nor yet some form beneath us.

St. John of the Cross – treated to a lengthy chapter in the third volume of *Herrlichkeit* – is perhaps the greatest purifier of form in the Western tradition. He insists that we place no credence whatever on forms revealed to us – on inner visions – nor on words spoken to us – on locutions. Not because God does not reveal Himself to us in them, but because we are so readily tricked by the illusions of the Devil, who also uses forms. Rather, God is greater than we are. If we cooperate with Him, He will prevail in our lives and will confirm what He is trying to convey to us – but for our own spiritual safety, we must ignore the seeming sensible data.

In a charming way, St. Teresa teased St. John about his suspicion of revealing form, noting that Our Lord had indeed made Himself very visible and tangible to Mary Magdalene, or to His Mother – and Balthasar would tend to agree with her more trusting stance. Again, this rests on the belief that God has chosen to create a world that says something important about Himself. And that God has chosen to come into this world Himself, to take on human form. Human form thus becomes a vehicle for God's self-expression: how ungrateful of us to ignore this, or to shy away from it in excessive caution! In the end, Balthasar knows that St. John of the Cross not only knows this, but magnificently celebrates it in his poetry: passionate lover of Christ Incarnate, Balthasar celebrates St. John as "poet of the night." But he walks a very narrow way between his poet's love of form and the mystic's apophatic insistence that our perception of form be purified.

God's Words

But can things, can created things, speak to us of God? And then, at a deeper level, can God make Himself known to us? Has He?

Taking his figure from St. Irenaeus, Balthasar writes of the three speeches of God: Creation, Scripture, and Incarnation. In the final one, in Jesus, God has fully and finally revealed Himself.

Balthasar insists that the beauty of Creation speaks to us of unseen depths:

> The form as it appears to us is beautiful only because the delight that it arouses in us is founded upon the fact that, in it, the truth and goodness of the depths of reality itself are manifested and bestowed, and this manifestation and bestowal reveal themselves to us as being something infinitely and inexhaustibly valuable and fascinating.[9]

Beyond Creation, once God has chosen to enter the world – the Incarnation – the rest of the story tells itself, as it were. Because this is a world of death, of fallenness, in His Body He takes up into Himself all the story of the world, from the first words of creation to the last words of any human death. And it is there that God utters the word beyond, a word that has not in fact ever been heard. That word is Resurrection, central truth of the Catholic faith, central mystery of the many mysteries. Indeed, Balthasar will link the Resurrection with the aesthetic way itself.

Anticipating what he will write elsewhere about the power of negative theology, Balthasar writes that:

> If there were no such thing as the resurrection of the flesh, then the truth would lie with gnosticism and every

form of idealism down to Schopenhauer and Hegel, for whom the finite must literally perish if it is to become spiritual and infinite. But the resurrection of the flesh vindicates the poets in a definitive sense: the aesthetic scheme of things, which allows us to possess the infinite within the finitude of form (however it is seen, understood or grasped spiritually), is right.[10]

But this "aesthetic scheme of things" which characterized the Catholic world, and indeed, the entire ancient world, has been disassociated from theology for centuries.[11]

The Great Divorce:
What Happened to the Beauty of Revelation

The living truth of the Catholic Faith was, of course, known and handed down through the ages in the Church. But the living contact with these "saving mysteries" was, Balthasar would say, dangerously obscured within the world of theology. In fact, he maintains, beauty became the lost transcendental.

The heart of the passion of his work is beauty, but a transcendental beauty which is more properly called "glory."

Glory, *Herrlichkeit – Slava* in the languages of much of Eastern Christianity: the search for what happened to the lost transcendental drives Balthasar's efforts. We find the word "glory" – *kabod, doxa* – running like a broad current throughout the Bible, both Old and New Testaments: the Glory of the Lord at the Ark, or on Mount Sinai; the Glory of the Lord at the Jerusalem Temple. In the New Testament, the angels sing their "*Gloria*" at the birth of Jesus, and His glory is seen on Mount Tabor, and then – He speaks of the glory to be revealed in His death, and His resurrection.

Yet what became of this glory in modern, Western Christianity? It was in fact something palpable to the people of the Bible: how else could they have known that, at the destruction of the Temple, the Glory of the Lord had left Israel?

A poet might say that glory is the splendor thrown off at the encounter of God with His world. God's supreme work of art is Jesus: and here, in the perfect wedding of God with the summit of His creation, man, glory radiates from the Incarnate One, even as it had hovered over the loci of holiness in the Old Testament. But now it is a glory that will shine through the wounds of the Cross. In the Johannine spirit, the Cross and the Glory are one. For Balthasar, the

Christian form is the most beautiful thing in the human realm: the beautiful form above all others is that of the saint, whose beauty – that is, form and splendor – participates in that of the supreme beauty, Christ.[12] Yet Balthasar sees that over time, Western Christian theology has failed to keep alive the central vision of the glory of God. Why?

The suspicion of a vision of glory goes back at least to the time of Montanism; in the first pages of the first volume of *Herrlichkeit*, Balthasar takes Ronald Knox's *Enthusiasm* to task on this issue.[13] For it is precisely enthusiasm that the encounter with God requires.

He traces the loss of this hunger for experience to an over-reaction at the time of Montanus on the part of the hierarchical Church, which led to an over-reliance on the valid principle of *"ex opere operato"* in which the principle, rather than being a safeguard of validity in the face of human weakness, was used as a block against an insistence on personal holiness and on personal experience of the things of God. In a word, vision is lacking.

Looking broadly at the various traditions, Balthasar intuits that the Catholic tradition, in recent centuries at least, had focused greatly on the truth: yet not daring to join St. Thomas in ascending to vision (that last step, to beauty), many in the Church contented themselves with articulating the intellectual articles, the cathedral vaults and arches – which yet were there to support the beauty of the stained glass windows, through which light was to enter. Perhaps we could say that discursive reason became increasingly severed from its grounding in intellectual vision, tending to become merely instrumental and technical.

The Protestant tradition, begun in a hunger for moral righteousness and an iconoclastic rejection of visible form, surrendered more and more to a preoccupation with the good, with the moral life, at the expense of both the true and the good.

The Eastern Church tended to become the primary repository of the Glory, as seen in the liturgy; even as its spirituality focused greatly on vision, the Taboric light. But this itself could become just a living museum of a glory once seen, and celebrated "gloriously" – yet somehow missing the living contact with the living God and living humanity. Although this overemphasis on the liturgy was countered in the Eastern tradition by a radical monasticism, still that tradition, focusing on the Taboric Light, has run the risk of becoming, and at times has become, a spiritually technologized Gnosis, an a-historical ontologism that sees the Cross dissolve in the light of the Resurrection.

Looking at the sweep of Christian history, Balthasar notes that the greatest tragedy in the history of Christianity was not any of the great ruptures – the Great Schism of 1054, or the Protestant Reformation of the 16th century – but rather the split between a "kneeling" and a "sitting" theology[14] – the gradual divorce between head and heart, which has led us to a visionless theology, and a mindless spirituality.[15]

This is particularly noteworthy in our age, when those who seek experience in the things of God have often been led into other religious traditions, because of the fierce limitations placed on the legitimate human need for experience when it is forced into an overly rationalized straight jacket. This has led to the phenomenon of the charismatic renewal, which has at times only fueled traditional suspicions by an anti-intellectualism in the name of a spiritual enthusiasm; it has fueled a craving for visions and apparitions apart from mainstream Church life; at another level, it has led many to a religious syncretism in search of religious experience. That which hearts are made for is all too often excluded in a Church of "talking heads" (and, more often than not, bitterly arguing heads!).

As we have seen, Bathasar pointedly noted that the person who no longer knew beauty would soon lose the ability to pray and to love as well. I have long pondered this prophetic observation of Balthasar's. It is interesting that the editor of an American Catholic magazine, adopting a rather critical stance toward mysticism while propounding a rather bellicose conceptualism, declared that Balthasar's statement was "the wildest exaggeration" he had ever heard[16] (speaking of exaggeration!). But without beauty, prayer and charity do diminish; hearts cannot be judged, but fruits can be. And the current state of internecine Church war speaks to this lack of a common focus of love. The Orthodox, for all their dissensions, yet find a common life in the one worship.[17] If imperfect, it yet points to something very precious that perhaps we in the West have lost.

There is a need for a rehabilitation of beauty as a legitimate, indeed, revealed, locus of encounter with God. So Balthasar seeks a theological aesthetics – not, let it be noted, an aesthetic theology.

He recalls antiquity's focus on the form and on its splendor – the two poles of an object's beauty. He must answer modernity's concerns with the perceiver of the beauty, most particularly those of Kant, by proposing a theory of perception. He faces a situation in which the Church has a formal word about God, in the Scripture and tradition, which had been presented syllogistically in the manual theology of his own early theological formation, the practical implications of which are spelled out in moral theology: lots of ideas. Feeding into this, like an illustration, is the mystical – which is yet kept carefully at the edges of things, a dangerous sort of fire, which yet is the only source of light and life.

Recent Centuries

We began by noting that beauty can be dangerous: this is much more the case when aligned with questions of experience and of mysticism in religion. No less a figure than St. Ignatius Loyola wrote in a letter[18] (included in William Meissner's psychological biography of the saint) that 90% of that which people think of as religious/mystical experience is false.

Much of Catholic theology is by no means alone in its suspicion of mysticism. The Protestant tradition, only heightened in its liberal development, has a strong history of hostility to the mystical – the German theological pun that mysticism comes from the two words "mist," or manure, and "schism" – witnesses to this.

And yet Balthasar dares to hold that what we consider "mysticism" was in fact the common experience of Christians throughout the ages. Recall the "experience" of a Benediction in a packed Church before the Vatican Council.

To rehabilitate the perception of beauty as a foundational entry into the knowledge of God, Balthasar explores at length how the contemplative perception of form was banished from its place at the heart of the science of theology: "Protestantism has pursued this excising of aesthetics from theology from the beginning, with Luther,"[19] whose stance Balthasar characterizes as "actualistic and ... anti-contemplative."[20] Beginning with Luther's "whore reason,"[21] and moving through Kierkegaard's profound suspicion of the aesthetic in religion – Kierkegaard contrasted the "genius" of art with religion,[22] the "apostle" and "martyr of truth" – *eros* has nothing to do with *agape*. To wed the ascending love of humanity with "the pure, descending love" ("Come, Oh Thou Traveler yet Unknown") is little less than blasphemy, as Anders Nygren would write from the Lutheran tradition. Every attempt at harmonizing divinity and humanity is smashed in an increasingly shrill Protestant dialectic. This might well be what lies behind much contemporary hostility to Balthasar's project:

> The word 'aesthetic' automatically flows from the pens of both Protestant and Catholic writers when they want to describe an attitude which, in the last analysis, they find to be frivolous, merely curious and self-indulgent.[23]

Kierkegaard's stance was further developed in the work of Emil Brunner, who:

> ... develops Kierkegaard's polemical schema of opposites into a methodological theological opposition between contemplative 'mysticism' and prophetic and Biblical faith in the Word.[24]

Spiritually, Protestantism thus became "full of anguish because of its total lack of imagery and form," something Balthasar calls a "real dead end for Protestantism."

To let beauty speak to us of God, in a way that allows God to remain God, we must invoke the fundamental Catholic principle of analogy, something which Karl Barth refused to do, initially, at least – calling analogy the "principle of the anti-Christ," and the one "greatest reason, if there were others lacking, for not becoming a Catholic."[25]

Yet Barth and Balthasar became close collaborators – it was the music of Mozart that brought them together, that is, beauty – and in the end, it seems, Barth did modify his strong anti-analogical sentiments. And, "at the conclusion of his treatment of the doctrine of the divine perfections," Barth restores "to God the attribute of 'beauty' for the first time in the history of Protestant theology."[26] Hence, Barth's significance for Balthasar's enterprise. Alas, as Balthasar notes, Barth's "contemplation of the objective revelation" has not yet transformed Protestant theology, which "continues in dutiful subservience to Bultmann's dualism of criticism, on the one hand, and existential, imageless inwardness, on the other."[27]

Analogy allows us to take this world seriously as a revelation of God without turning it into an idol: analogy gives us the right proportions with which to treat forms/images/words as pointers to God, saying something about Him; but, as is the nature with analogical language in the things of God, being is always ultimately inadequate to the task.[28]

Moving toward the Catholic vision, Balthasar characterizes the central act of theology as a science in terms of the Augustinian *"fruitio"*[29] – an experience of enjoyment and delight in the spiritual sense of Scripture. That enjoyment should take the "place of honor" in the science of theology, but it is banished in most modern theologies, Protestant and Catholic. For theology, there is a "real and inescapable obligation to probe the possibility of there being a genuine relationship between theological beauty and the beauty of the world."[30] Once again, analogy – the key to the uniquely Catholic sacramental vision – is crucial.

And the perception of beauty is at the heart of any true reading of the Scriptures:

> True exegesis means: to move to the point where the image (*das Bild*), in the Spirit, becomes transparent of him who made the image (*der Bildende*), and this 'maker of images' is God and man in unity. For such exegesis historical expertise is, of course, needed; but to a far greater extent there is required the divining power of imaginative reconstruction – that youth of the heart which is able to feel at one with the historical and eternal youth of mankind.[31]

Thus, scandalous as it may seem, "Scholarly enquiry must become contemplation."[32]

What is it the scholar is to contemplate? It is a revealed form.

Image – form – is the very heart of divine revelation. Balthasar favors the poet and theologian, Johann Gottfried Herder, disciple of Johann Georg Hamann, for whom the Bible as a whole was poetry, "and may, therefore, be reconstructed only as a world of images."[33] Herder also supplies Balthasar with a favorite notion – that "as man and woman, the human being is 'a moving image'"[34] of God.

The great enemy for Balthasar is what we might call a "bad infinity," a negative "void" which would seem to liberate us from difficult, often antagonistic, positions created by a theistic vision. And that liberates us from any image, any form, any individual being. In spite of the Zen tradition's clear warning about imagining any void, taking their lead from Kyoto school thinkers like Masao Abe, inter-religious dialoguers frequently seek refuge from the problem of God precisely in the concept of "the void." And that means, at the very least, a radical apophaticism beyond all forms and images.

The mystic Meister Eckhart is a favorite in these approaches, but for Balthasar, there is no Eckhartian Godhead behind God. The Father *is* God, the source of God-hood; and Jesus is the fullness of the revelation of God. Not just that which God chose to reveal, as if there were a dark side of the moon, while Jesus was the illumined face. No: "He who has seen me has seen the Father," and there is nothing held back in Jesus. God has been seen in the form of Christ, and it is a permanent form, one that is able to reveal God fully.

God can reveal and has revealed Himself fully in Christ.

The Beauty of Christ

Yet what is the beauty of the form in Jesus? Is he more beautiful than Adonis? Why did Michelangelo make a David but not a Jesus for us to admire in the Academia?

Rainer Maria Rilke wrote that "beauty is nothing but the beginning of the terrible."[35] The beauty in Jesus is one that "was marred," one that, being truly beautiful, was also somehow terrible. In the hauntingly beautiful Suffering Servant passages, the mysterious passages where Balthasar sees the uniqueness of the New Testament revelation suddenly, unaccountably emerging in the middle of the Old Testament, we find a prophecy of one whose beauty is not of this world. In fact, it is a face we would not notice, and even that face was marred.

How could this face be most beautiful?

There is a passage in French author Jean Sulivan's *Eternity, My Beloved*[36] where Strozzi, the obedient but marginalized priest who works in Paris's underworld, comes upon the body of a lesbian who had attempted suicide in a stuffy bourgeois Catholic apartment. Enraged by a religion that had prettified the Crucified and rendered Him ineffective in this woman's life, Father Strozzi leaps up and tears down the ivory corpus which is encased above the mantel and smashes it. Beauty did not save, for it was a beauty that betrayed the crucified. The corpus represents the opposite of that transcending beauty which is glory, and which is revealed on the Cross: the ivory corpus is less than the glory of God, and cheapens the sacrifice of Christ, rendering it ineffective, merely beautiful, merely "*bello.*"[37] Chesterton, perceiving the same tendency, castigates other traditions for turning the once angular Cross into an object of almost Gnostic symmetry, as in the Eastern Church.

Sacred art must be in harmony with the God who is above our ideas of harmony, Whose Cross shatters our human aesthetics and opens to the divine beauty, for "art's fruitful womb is the soul's attunedness to God."[38] Again, analogy rules.

The aesthetics of the Cross is not one of symmetry, but rather, one which breaks symmetry – and yet within, there is a beauty bursting into the world along with a cry of pain which shatters all the canons of art, which dwarfs mere aestheticism and replaces it with the beauty of God made man. Here, Truth and Goodness are in fact one with Beauty, but that beauty is penetrating, not skin deep, deeper than the very blood in the marrow. This beauty must draw others into its embrace. Sent from the heart of Glory into the darkened world, the one on whom the glory of God shone came to graft others onto His life.

Life Form

And so we have discipleship. Was Mary – the all-beautiful one, the dwelling place of god's glory, the new temple, the greatest of all the disciples – more beautiful in fact than the most beautiful of women? Than a Venus? A difficult question, but Balthasar might answer with a citation from Rilke that he particularly liked: in his "Archaic Torso of Apollo," Rilke wrote: "There is no place in it that does not see you. You must change your life."[39] That is, you have gone out of yourself in an ecstasy to the beautiful and lost self-consciousness: you are seen, and then aware of being seen by something transcending your world. And this is the basis for conversion, this is the basis for moral action. Action "in the light."

Life: and a life form. It is this, ultimately, of which Balthasar is writing. An *eros* which draws, which pulls to the source of beauty in a human face, a human body and soul, that of Jesus. And drawn to Him, one is sent out from Him, as He was, on mission, the mission of kneading the form of Christ into the life of His disciple. The supreme artistry of God is to take recalcitrant human spirit-matter, and, in and through His Beloved Son, to turn a wounded, self-preoccupied puddle of egotism into an independent, free being who finds its glory in willing the death of his own self that the Beloved might take up residence in him.

True beauty, then, summons to holiness. It is the wedding of form and splendor, and it speaks; the splendor reaches out and transforms, if one is willing to be "*entrückt,*" enraptured by it. One must experience this "ecstasy," one must leave everything behind, one must be willing to be lifted out of oneself and placed into union with the other. Otherwise, like the rich young man whom Jesus loved, one just walks away sad.

The ultimate beauty is that perfect self-giving revealed in the bleeding wounds of Christ: an endlessly drawing stream of life, a mutual ecstasy of selflessness pouring out from the Cross, pouring down into the world from the Trinity.

Consequences of the Crucified Beauty

The disciples who allow themselves to be captured by the other-beauty of Jesus become saints who radiate His beauty into the world. Balthasar has written that the saint is the best apology for the Christian religion, and this is certainly borne out for me after many years in the classroom. I begin each "Introduction to Theology" class with Malcolm Muggeridge's biography of Mother Teresa in an attempt to deflect my students from their chorus of "I'm Catholic, but disagree on issues like women priests, abortion, homosexuality, and contraception."

But "unless you turn and become as little children you cannot enter the Kingdom of Heaven." It is the task of the artist to turn from the ways of seeing that characterize the mass of humanity ("the way is broad") and to listen to the different drummer. He shares this task with the saint. Perhaps one major difference, however, between artist and saint is that the artist must focus on his own experience, and so on himself, whereas, for Balthasar, the saint goes beyond. The saint renounces self in an effort to become more and more transparent to Christ's light radiating through him or her. Again, analogy rightly orders understanding.

Much is said today of the failures of contemporary catechesis. As a teacher, I am painfully aware of this.[40] The worst blow, though, is not from the students who claim to have had many years of Catholic education and know nothing of the faith. It comes rather from those who in fact get straight A's on their quizzes; who know the facts of a catechism back and forth; and yet who are totally untouched – in fact, who are often hostile and resentful. The fact is, they have not "seen the form." They have been "taught" by teachers who themselves have not learned to see, and so the form does not emerge from the jumble of facts which without the magnet of form are nothing more than fragments of truth, material for a "Catholic trivia" game. Anything less than seeing the form trivializes Him: and it trivializes the price He paid that we might see.

It is commonly known that Dostoyevsky once wrote that "the world will be saved by beauty." We have come to that age: a visual, symbol-oriented age, which needs to recover its heart before it can recover its head. Balthasar has written that though the Church has sanctioned devotion to the Sacred Heart, there is no devotion to the sacred head except when it is bloodied and covered with thorns. The divine *eros* has reached down to us through the blood of that head and heart, drawing the best of us to contemplate – in awesome wonder – this work that God has made, this work that God has become. His *eros*, called *agape* by us, elicits a response from the deepest part of ourselves, that longs to see a beloved face emerge from the vast spaces of the universe. As Balthasar never tired of pointing out, that face is as far as heaven, and as near as the needy neighbor, revealed in Christ Jesus. Contemplating that face, we will be able again to build beautiful churches. More: in union with the all-beautiful one who "kept all these things in her heart,"(Lk. 2:51), we will be able to become a beautiful church, gathered at the foot of His Cross, born ever anew from His loving and luminous wound.

Father Raymond Gawronski, S.J., is currently an Assistant Professor of Theology at Marquette University. He received an S.T.D. in Systematics from the Gregorian University in Rome in 1992. He specializes in dogmatic theology, with a focus on the mystical, and on eschatology, particularly as articulated in the work of Hans Urs von Balthasar. The latter's understanding of the Catholic spiritual heritage in the encounter with world religions is the subject of Father Gawronski's book, *Word and Silence: Hans Urs von Balthasar and the Spiritual Encounter between East and West.* Balthasar's theology of the saints as "living apologies" for Christianity, and the question of redemptive suffering, are particular interests of his.

Almost thirty articles by Father Gawronski on various themes, especially those touching upon spirituality and culture, have appeared in publications such as *Communio, New Oxford Review,* and *America*; he also authored the chapter on *"Redemptor Hominis"* in *The Thought of John Paul II.* He is currently working on an existential commentary on the *Spiritual Exercises* of Saint Ignatius of Loyola, which will accompany his video series on the same topic. See also his talk "When Beauty Is Revolutionary: Reflections on *Liturgiam Authenticam"* among the Special Conference Session talks later in this volume.

Notes

1 John Saward, *The Beauty of Holiness and the Holiness of Beauty: Art, Sanctity, and the Truth of Catholicism* (San Francisco: Ignatius Press, 1996), p. 36.

2 Heinrich Zimmer, *Philosophies of India* (Cleveland NY: Meridian Books, The World Publishing Company, 1951), p. 52, note 7, distinguishes the two concepts in a passage about concentration of the mind: "Exercises of meditation on the worshiper's special tutelary divinity (*istadevata*), which is an 'aspect-provided-with-qualities' (*sa-guna*) of the highest essence (*brahman*). *Brahman* in itself is absolutely devoid of qualifications (*nir-guna*), and consequently beyond the reach of the powers of the normal human mind. The various *istadevatas*, images, and personifications consequently, are only preliminary helps, guides, or accommodations, which serve to prepare the spirit of the worshiper for its final, form-transcending realization."

3 Anthony de Mello, *Sadhana: A Way to God* (St. Louis: The Institute of Jesuit Sources, 1978), p. 26.

4 The Ignatian tradition differs from much if not most in other Christian as well as world mystical traditions by using the imagination to enter into communion with God, not as a preliminary step, but as the proper response to a God who speaks in words and images. We shall return to this shortly.

5 *Glory* I, p. 18.

6 "A metaphysics that in the modern world has "run aground on the sandbanks of a technological rationalism" (from Breandan Leahy, "Theological Aesthetics" in *The Beauty* of *Christ*, ed. Bede McGregor, O.P. and Thomas Norris, Edinburgh: T&T Clark Ltd. 1994, p. 28).

7 Joseph Cardinal Ratzinger, *The Beauty of the Liturgy,* towards p. 200.

8 Joseph Cardinal Ratzinger, *Introduction to Christianity* (NY: Crossroad Publishing Company, 1985), chapter 1.

9 *Glory* I, p. 118.

10 *Glory* I, p. 155.

11 Both Balthasar (*Glory* II) and John Saward (*The Beauty of Holiness and the Holiness of Beauty*) begin their volumes with a citation from the same work of Francis Thompson: "The Church, which was once the mother of poets no less than of saints, during the last two centuries has relinquished to aliens the chief glories of poetry, if the chief glories of holiness she has preserved for her own"; "...she has retained the palm, but forgone the laurel." ("Once poetry was, as she should be, the lesser sister and help-mate of the Church; the minister to the mind, as the Church to the soul. But poetry sinned, poetry fell; and in place of lovingly reclaiming her, Catholicism cast her from the door to follow the feet of her pagan seduc-er. The separation has been ill for poetry; it has not been well for reli-gion." Cardinal Ratzinger, in the preface to Saward's book, writes: "[Christians] must make their Church into a place where beauty – and hence truth – is at home. Without this the world will become the first cir-cle of hell."

12 Hans Urs von Balthasar, *The Glory of the Lord: A Theological Aesthetics,* Vol. I, *Seeing the Form,* tr. Erasmo Leiva-Merikakis (San Francisco: Ignatius Press, 1982), p. 28. Henceforth: *Glory* I.

13 *Glory* I, p. 40.

14 See his article "Theology and Holiness," in *Explorations in Theology* I: The *Word Made Flesh,* tr. A.V. Littledale with Alexander Dru (San Francisco: Ignatius Press, 1989).

15 Breandan Leahy, p. 34: "If beauty were to be bracketed off, then the good and truth lose their evidence and are no longer binding."

16 Editorial and letter, *New Oxford Review*, Berkeley, Ca. June 2001. "You are swimming in dangerous currents," the editor writes, "even in your appeal to mysticism, for as Fr. Alexander Schmemann warned, mysti-cism all too often 'begins in mist and ends in schism.'"

17 In an article in *America* magazine in the summer of 2001 (July 30–Aug. 6, 2001, Vol. 185, No. 3, p. 19) addressing those Catholics who would weaken magisterial authority in favor of a unity located in shared liturgy, as the Orthodox have putatively known it, Archbishop Charles Chaput sadly observes that all Catholics would have to acknowledge that after the on-going battles of the past decades, the Latin Catholic liturgy could not today serve as such a point of unity.

18 See William W. Meissner, *Ignatius of Loyola: The Psychology of a Saint* (Yale University Press, 1994).

19 *Glory* I, p. 26.

20 *Ibid.,* p. 57.

21 *Ibid.*

22 *Ibid.,* p. 50.

23 *Ibid.,* p. 51.

24 *Ibid.,* p. 52.

25 *Ibid.*

26 *Ibid.*

27 *Ibid.*, p. 56.

28 Balthasar frequently recalls the Fourth Lateran Council: "*...inter creatorem et creaturam non potest similitudo notari, quin inter eos maior sit dissimilitudo notanda*" Denziger-Schoenmetzer, 806.

29 *Ibid.*, p. 76.

30 *Ibid.*, pp. 79–80.

31 *Ibid.*, p. 85.

32 *Ibid.*, p. 102.

33 *Ibid.*, p. 84.

34 *Ibid.*, pp. 84–85.

35 Rainer Maria Rilke, as cited in *Glory* I, p. 65.

36 Jean Sulivan, *Eternity*, My *Beloved* tr. Sr. Francis Ellen Riordan (St. Paul, Minn.: River Boat Books, 1998). (French original, 1966).

37 For those with any familiarity with Italian Catholicism, the problem of the merely "pretty" – "*che bello!*" – in religion will be readily called to mind.

38 Glory I, p. 99.

39 As quoted in *Glory* I, p. 23.

40 I have just been grading undergraduate quizzes, to discover – yet again – that Christ was "killed in Calgary."

Chapter 3
Response to Father Raymond Gawronski's Paper on the Theological Aesthetics of Hans Urs Von Balthasar
Larry Chapp

I would like to begin by thanking Fr. Gawronski for his very fine paper on Balthasar's aesthetics. I have spent the better part of the past 16 years attempting to encapsulate Balthasar's theology in order to explain it to the Balthasarian neophyte, so I know how difficult a project it is. I think Fr. Gawronski has succeeded admirably, and so in my comments this evening, I will not try to rehearse all over again the same territory he has so admirably scoped. Instead, I would like to focus on one aspect of Balthasar's aesthetics and explore a little further some of its implications for modern theology. I would also like to add the following reassurance: my remarks will be brief.

It has always been my firm conviction that the quickest path to understanding the inner ethos of great thinkers is to ask a very simple question: what is it that he or she most feared? Why did they write what they did in the manner that they did? What was their inner motivation? What were they trying to avoid? Prophetically, what trends in contemporary thought did they presciently view as dangerous and full of portent? Often, the best way to read the entire opus of a great thinker is to view the whole enterprise as a cautionary tale – "Look out! Here is what you must avoid!" And that is what I propose to do now, in response to Fr. Gawronski's paper – to address the question of why Balthasar developed his theological aesthetic in the first place. My comments, therefore, should be viewed as an extended commentary on Fr. Gawronski's observation that Balthasar viewed the split between theology and sanctity, or theology and mysticism, as the greatest tragedy to befall theology, and the one reality that must be avoided or remedied at all costs. In particular, I want to emphasize what Balthasar viewed as the tragic turn of theology to the Enlightenment's spirit of critical abstraction – the hegemony of *"Begriff"* or "Rational Concept" over the entire theological enterprise – and the consequent marginalization of the contemplative in an overwhelming ocean of dialectic. What is under indictment, in other words, is the very spirit of critical theology itself. As Balthasar scans the landscape of modern theology, he fears a growing loss of a sense of the whole, an inability to perceive the "form" of God's revelation as a thing that I should delight in and in whose ambient light I am bathed. Balthasar says that a great work of art can become *"geistlos"* over time when it is viewed repeatedly by those who do not have the eye to see it in its true form and beauty. What Balthasar fears is that the spirit of modern critical theology is rendering Revelation as *geistlos*, thus explaining why it no longer seems attractive, a thing to be desired, by the modern world. Thus, the entire Balthasarian project can be viewed as an attempt at the repristination of revelation in a world that has lost its ability to see. Thus, Balthasar's project is as much about our inability to see as it is about God's revelation as such.

Balthasar is fond of quoting Lessing and sees in him the quintessence of the Enlightenment's approach to religion. Lessing's dictum was that historical-contingent events were inadequate vessels for the timeless and universal truths of reason. You simply cannot get a universally valid religion out of the Bible's contingent historical revelation. In the wake of this critique, critical philosophy will question the validity of a historical revelation that claims immunity from the hermeneutical circle. Propositional models for revelation are discredited as invalid attempts to universalize an inherently time-bound and culture-bound historical reality.

Nor, in a sense, does one escape the problem through a Lindbeckian appeal to the normative status of an interpretive tradition – for even in a normative tradition rooted in experience, one must acknowledge that error and distortion have entered into the tradition. Therefore, the so-called "hermeneutics of suspicion" engages in the deconstruction of the once-normative tradition in order to reconstruct it along the lines of modernity's canons of rationality. Liberal theology is thus characterized by a deep distrust for the historical particularity of revelation and an even deeper distrust of the particularities of the ecclesial mediation of that Revelation. In short, liberal theology is marked by Lessing's profound agnosticism with regard to the ability of the contingent to express the universal. Hence, the constant liberal quest to distill the essence of revelation by boiling away the various "media" of revelation (Scripture, Church, etc.) in the heat of critical abstraction in order to discover finally the residue of truth left behind – this is the hallmark of our age and the legacy of the Enlightenment.

In sum, then, it can be said that reductionist critical exegesis of the Bible and the hermeneutics of suspicion applied to the tradition have destroyed the ability of both to act as a suitable medium for divine revelation. For the liberal critical theologian, revelation, if it continues on as a viable concept at all, does so only as an idealist abstraction – an abstraction that loses its rational warrant and actually undergoes a declension as it fights its way through the opaqueness of historical mediation. The task of the theologian in this scheme is to catalogue the nature of the declension of revelation in its various historical mediations. This is accomplished in various theological specializations whose sole task seems to be the removal of the part from the whole in order to isolate it for proper analysis – a kind of theological forensics that has all the air of a post-mortem. In this context I would like to offer a quote from the late Allan Bloom on the relationship between specialization and this spirit of critical abstraction:

> A specialist cuts off an aspect of the whole of things man faces, orders it, and becomes competent at dealing with it. The doctor or the engineer appeals to us on the basis of what might be called the charm of competence. Specialists represent an important and dignified human temptation, one in which the quest for knowledge is fulfilled as in no other domain. They can make claims to rational demonstration that those who want to face the whole cannot rival. They are good at reasoning except about the whole and their own place in it. This abstraction of a part from the whole provides intelligibility, but at the sacrifice of the erotic aspiration for completeness and self-discovery. The specialist lacks or suppresses such longing. Specialization is an attempt to make things utterly transparent and susceptible to rational analysis. But they have a tendency to resist reflection on the relationship of this abstract

science to the world in which men actually live (Allan Bloom, *Love and Friendship*, p. 470).

Along similar lines, Balthasar quotes Bernanos with approval on the subject of "intellectual systems": "I have no system, because the systematic spirit is a form of madness. Systems are good only for madmen. Common sense teaches us that by pretending to simplify, systems complicate everything, while life itself, while seeming to complicate, in fact simplifies everything" (Balthasar, *Bernanaos*, pp. 37–38).

What becomes very clear in Balthasar is his rejection of this spirit of critical abstraction and its kissing cousin – the hyper-specialization of modern theology. This is what Balthasar means by "the System" in his polemical text *Cordula oder der Ernstfall*, a text that retains its importance despite its polemics. And that is why he agrees with Bernanos' equating of "the System" with madness. The purpose of specialization in the liberal scheme is not to view *Das Ganze im Fragment* – the whole *in* the fragment – but to dissolve the fragment's particularity – not into a "whole" conceived of as a Gestalt – but into the nothingness of nihilism, or the overarching control of an abstract rationality that Balthasar describes as a form of titanistic, egoistic grasping. Here one is reminded of Dostoevsky's Inquisitor – a bloodless man possessed of a corpse-like lifelessness who places the Lord of life in the dank prison of his cold abstractions. Balthasar views critical-liberal theology as a similarly desiccated enterprise incapable of the contemplative posture required to grasp the form, the *Gestalt*, of God's Revelation in Christ.

We can therefore say with some confidence that it is proper to characterize Balthasar's theology as post-critical and post-liberal (I refuse to say "postmodern" because I am not certain anyone really knows what that term means). He is critical of the liberal love for abstraction – after all, the abstraction itself is just as historically contingent, just as culturally conditioned and time-bound as any other historical artifact. Thus, Balthasar correctly sees the latent atheism in the liberal-critical project. Schleiermacher, for example, appeals to human religious experience as the locus of divine revelation in order to ground the latter in the realm of the empirical – religiously altered consciousness which can, after all, be scientifically studied. He thought this gave religious experience and revelation a sure footing in something that could be remotely described as reason. And yet, how do we know that our feelings of absolute dependence or our intuitions are really encounters with God? How do we escape the Feuerbachian critique that God is a projection of our religious feelings? How do we avoid Freud's critique? In the end, we have no intra-mundane warrant for positing God as the source of these experiences.

This also seems to be the basis for Balthasar's critique of Rahner. The turn to the subject, the desire to ground revelation in an anthropological dynamism, in the end, freights our inner experience of the "always more" of our consciousness with a weight it simply cannot bear. In short, the liberal attempt to evade the problems associated with the rejection of historical particularity by retreating into the realm of "praxis" or "experience" or "existential authenticity" is a self-contradicting move that eventually leads to the rejection of experience as a ground for revelation, leaving atheism as the only living alternative. Liberal theology cannot escape from the bogeyman of its own creation and leads, by an inner inexorable logic, to the nihilism Nietzsche so presciently described as being at the very heart of the liberal, bourgeois project like a ticking time bomb.

Thus, I think the value of Balthasar's aesthetics for modern theology – so ably described by Fr. Gawronski – is its insistence upon a reversal of the entire liberal project. What this means in the concrete is an abandonment of the spirit of critical-abstraction and its concomitant distrust of the historical and contingent. It also means the rejection of the hyper-specialization of theology that has the effect of embedding in the very typology of the discipline an implied methodology – no attempt at seeing the Whole, the Form, the *Gestalt* will be made because no attempt can be made. All are fearful of appearing as hopeless dilettantes or as interlopers into the domain of others or, at worst, as naïve fools who do not understand the latest findings in this or that discipline. We stand paralyzed in fear before the specter of the theological specialist who stands ready to rap our knuckles if we dare claim knowledge outside of our own biodome.

Thus, I think Fr. Gawronski is utterly correct when he points out that "For Balthasar, everything comes down to the question: Is there a God, and then, has He said anything of Himself?" Indeed. The God of Jesus Christ is a God who speaks. Balthasar's challenge to modern theology is radical because it is simple: Do we have the expan-

sive contemplative sensibility to comprehend what this God is saying, or will we insist on subjecting God's self-unveiling to the
pinched restrictions of our Promethean suspicions?

Dr. Larry Chapp is Associate Professor of Theology and
Chairman of the Department of Philosophy and Theology at DeSales
University in Center Valley, Pennsylvania. He received his doctorate
from Fordham University in 1994 with a dissertation on Hans Urs
von Balthasar's theology of revelation. In 1996 he published a book
entitled *The God Who Speaks: Hans Urs von Balthasar's Theology
of Revelation.* He has written numerous articles in various journals.
Dr. Chapp is married with one daughter and lives in Coopersburg,
Pennsylvania.

Chapter 4
The Sacramental Vision of J.R.R. Tolkien
C. N. Sue Abromaitis

Given the complexity of the narrative of *The Hobbit* and the three parts of *The Lord of the Rings*, namely, *The Fellowship of the Rings, The Two Towers*, and *The Return of the King*, I will give a brief summary of events for those who have not read them. *The Hobbit* tells of the journey, *"There and Back Again,"* of Bilbo, a typical Hobbit, stay-at-home, comfortable, well-fed. Through the machinations and with the occasional protection of the wizard Gandalf, Bilbo leaves his beloved Shire and has adventures. He travels with a group of dwarves to help them reclaim their treasure held by an evil dragon (in Tolkien all dragons fulfill their archetypal role of being evil). In the course of the journey that in many ways is a rite of passage, Bilbo gains a magic ring that when worn makes him invisible. The trilogy begins sixty years later at Bilbo's party celebrating his eleventy-first birthday. Rather than a journey to find a treasure, the trilogy is a journey to destroy a treasure, the very ring that Bilbo found. In this journey, the rational creatures of Middle Earth – Wizards, the Dark Lord, Elves, Ents, the Nazgul, Men, Dwarves, Orcs, talking beasts and birds, Barrow-wights, and Hobbits – are engaged in a struggle that has cosmic significance. Most notable about these four books is the imagination that created their world.

That the imagination is of central importance for an authentic Catholic intellect is the premise of this conference. According to St. Thomas Aquinas "it is clear that for the intellect to understand actually, not only when it acquires new knowledge, but also when it uses knowledge already acquired, there is need for the act of the imagination."[1] Moreover, in his theory and practice, Pope John Paul II emphasizes imagination as a faculty that can ennoble, enrich, and enhance humanity. When philosophers and literary figures throughout the ages examine the nature and operations of the imagination, their presuppositions about what is real inform their analyses.

So too does J. R. R. Tolkien reflect upon imagination. He explicitly states that man, made in God's image and likeness, shares in the work of God's creation. At the same time Tolkien is quite aware of his being in a fallen world, one in which he is working against the *Zeitgeist*. This spirit of the age permeates the artistic depiction of man as the inevitably alienated stranger. The presumption of the age is, in a certain sense, a mixture of two apparently opposed concepts of the real: materialism, reducing all of reality to that which is sense perceptible, and Gnosticism, positing a spiritualistic reality available only to the *illuminati*. Visiting the South-bank Tate or MOMA; viewing current dramas, movies, and television shows; listening to contemporary music, whether atonal or rap; watching modern and postmodern dance; reading the latest literary criticism, art commentary, and fiction – all these things reveal how both mainstream and *avant garde* artists and critics adhere to a vision of the world which is materialistic and/or Gnostic. Their work essentially denies meaning and harmony, assumes that nothing can be known with certitude, and apotheosizes the self-consciously absurd, nihilistic, hedonistic, antiheroic, deterministic, and downright ugly. Meanwhile apologists for this art constitute a self-appointed *cognoscenti* who act as translators of the world and word for the unenlightened. Michael Medved describes the "power of entertainment industry ... to redefine what constitutes normal behavior ... [and to assume] a dominant role in establishing social conventions."[2] So the works of these artists and entertainers reflect the world and shape it.

Ranged against this horror is the sacramental vision that imbues Tolkien's *oeuvre*, sacramental because Tolkien sees in the world and its creatures the manifestation of God's love for man. And he asserts that "one object" of his literary creation is:

> ... the elucidation of truth, and the encouragement of good morals in this real world, by the ancient device of exemplifying them in unfamiliar embodiments, that may tend to "bring them home."[3]

His seriousness is a function of his awareness of God's love expressed in the goodness of creation. Clearly, he believes that all who will open themselves to the epiphanies that surround them can experience this goodness. Tolkien's literary theory and practice affirm the glorious reality of the world created by God, Who, as Gerard Manley Hopkins says, "fathers forth whose beauty is past change." Like Hopkins, Tolkien is counter-cultural because he too sees in the beauty of creation proof of the hallowed nature of man.

In one of his major theoretical works, the 1947 essay *On Fairy-Stories*, Tolkien asserts:

> The human mind is capable of forming mental images of things not actually present. The mental power of image making ...The perception of the image, the grasp of its implications, and the control, which are necessary to a successful expression, may vary in vividness and strength: but this is a difference of degree in Imagination, not a difference in kind.[4]

Tolkien "arrogates" to himself "the powers of Humpty-Dumpty": he uses Fantasy to mean "both the Sub-creative Art in itself and a quality of strangeness and wonder in the Expression, derived from the image" (*Tree*, 47). After an extensive analysis of the nature of Fantasy, the first of the four marks that "fairy-stories offer ... in a peculiar degree or mode" (*Tree*, 46), Tolkien concludes:

> Fantasy is a natural human activity. It certainly does not destroy or even insult Reason; and it does not either blunt the appetite for, nor obscure the perception of, scientific verity. On the contrary. The keener and clearer is the reason, the better Fantasy it will make. If men were ever in a state in which they did not want to know or could not perceive truth (facts or evidence), then Fantasy would languish until they were cured ...
>
> For creative Fantasy is founded upon the hard recognition that things are so in the world as it appears under the sun; on a recognition of fact, but not a slavery to it (*Tree*, 54–55).

Even as Tolkien defends Fantasy as a good thing, he does not ignore the evil uses to which it may be put:

> Fantasy can, of course, be carried to excess. It can be ill done. It can be put to evil uses. It may even delude the minds out of which it came. But of what human thing in this fallen world is that not true (*Tree*, 55).

In another context, he comments that:

> Great harm can be done, of course, by this potent mode of "myth" – especially willfully. The right to "freedom" of

the sub-creator is no guarantee among fallen men that it will not be used as wickedly as is Free Will. I am comforted by the fact that some, more pious and learned than I, have found nothing harmful in this Tale or its feigning as a "myth." ... [5]

His literary fantasy is not ill nor evil nor delusive because he sees his art as an expression of man's sacramental nature. He is using his God-given faculties by imitating Him in making. He asserts that this secondary creation is a good act "because we are made: and not only made, but made in the image and likeness of a Maker" (*Tree* 55).

Thus, his aesthetic is informed with the universal moral law even as Tolkien praises the goodness of Him Who created nature. Similarly, in his explanation of Recovery, the second mark of fairy-stories or *Marchen*, Tolkien's belief in objective reality that means itself and at the same time is a sign of something else is apparent.

Recovery (which includes return and renewal of health) is a re-gaining – regaining of a clear view. I do not say "seeing things as they are" and involve myself with the philosophers, though I might venture to say "seeing things as we are (or were) meant to see them" – as things apart from ourselves (*Tree*, 57).

These same premises are apparent in his discussion of the third quality, Escape. Tolkien defends it against the critics who disapprove of escape in literature by contending that he is speaking not of "the Flight of the Deserter," but of "the Escape of the Prisoner" (*Tree* 60). And the prison that he would have his readers escape is "the Robot Age, that combines elaboration and ingenuity of means with ugliness, and (often) with inferiority of result" (*Tree*, 61). After exploring the implications of Christopher Dawson's characterization of "the rawness and ugliness of modern European life" (*Tree*, 63), Tolkien comments that there is an attempt to escape from this ugly world in the stories of "Scientifiction." However, what these "prophets" create are worlds of "improved means to deteriorated ends" (*Tree* 64). Without an authentic teleology, theirs is an escape without a destination. Moreover, although modern man's recognition that "the ugliness of our works, and of their evil" are things to flee is apparently a good thing, it too often results in a serious misconception about beauty:

> [T]o us evil and ugliness seem indissolubly allied. We find it difficult to conceive of beauty together. The fear of the beautiful fay that ran through the elder ages almost eludes our grasp. Even more alarming: goodness is itself bereft of its proper beauty (*Tree*, 65).

Tolkien points out that the healthy perception that there is beauty that can lead man to hell has been lost in the modern world. The dreadful result of that loss is apparent in the deformed morality that pervades the modern age: if something is beautiful and, therefore, arouses my desire, it must be good for me to have it. Tolkien's analysis of the meaning and nature of the particular aesthetic embodiment of imagination in the fairy story is informed by a consistent rejection of the vulgarity of solipsism and relativism. These reflexes cause modern man to reject his sacramental nature. This rejection, in turn, accounts for the barrenness and joylessness so evident in modern art.

In contrast, as his discussion of the final mark of *Marchen* makes clear, Tolkien emphasizes joy. He asserts that "the Consolation of the Happy Ending ... *Eucatastrophe* ... is the true form of fairy-tale, and its highest function" (*Tree*, 68). He then explains:

> The consolation of fairy-stories, the joy of the happy ending: or more correctly of the good catastrophe, the sudden joyous "turn" ... one of the things which fairy-stories can produce supremely well, is not essentially "escapist," nor "fugitive." ... [I]t is a sudden and miraculous grace: never to be counted on to recur. It does not deny the existence of *dyscatastrophe*, of sorrow and failure: the possibility of these is necessary to the joy of deliverance; it denies (in the face of much evidence ...) universal final defeat and in so far is *evangelium*, giving a fleeting glimpse of Joy, Joy beyond the walls of the world, poignant as grief (*Tree*, 68).

In the Epilogue to the essay, Tolkien explicitly connects the Gospels with fairy stories:

> God redeemed the corrupt making-creatures, men, in a way fitting to this aspect, as to others, of their strange nature. The Gospels contain a fairy-story, or a story of a larger kind which embraces all the essence of fairy-stories. They contain many marvels – peculiarly artistic, beautiful, and moving ... among the marvels is the greatest and most

complete conceivable eucatastrophe. But this story has
entered History and the primary world; the desire and aspi-
ration of sub-creation has been raised to the fulfillment of
Creation. The Birth of Christ is the eucatastrophe of Man's
history. The Resurrection is the eucatastrophe of the story
of the Incarnation. This story begins and ends in joy (*Tree*
71–72).

Just as John Paul II's encyclical *Fides et Ratio*[6] insists that reason can only find its fulfillment in revelation,[7] so Tolkien makes the
same point about the relation between art and revelation: the Gospel
"is supreme; and it is true. Art has been verified" (*Tree*, 72). Just as
it is an inherent principle of creation that finite man use his reason,
so also does man's telling stories flow from the nature of creation:

> But in God's kingdom the presence of the greatest does
> not depress the small. Redeemed Man is still man. Story,
> Fantasy, still go on, and should go on. The Evangelium has
> not abrogated legends; it has hallowed them, especially the
> "happy ending." The Christian has still to work, with mind
> as well as body ... So great is the bounty with which he has
> been treated, that he may now, perhaps, fairly dare to guess
> that in Fantasy he may actually assist in the effoliation and
> multiple enrichment of creation (*Tree*, 73).

Such enrichment of the primary world is a great achievement.
That Tolkien had an early sense of being called to do significant
work is apparent in a 1916 letter to G. B. Smith,[8] in which he says
that each of the four friends in their schoolboy group was called to
be "a great instrument in God's hands – a mover, a doer, even an
achiever of great things, a beginner at the very least of large things."[9]
Moreover, he writes that all in the group:

> ... had been granted some spark of fire – certainly as a body
> if not singly – that was destined to kindle a new light, or,
> what is the same thing, rekindle an old light in the world;
> that ...[each one] was destined to testify for God and
> Truth.[10]

In reading Tolkien's works, particularly *The Lord of the Rings*,
one has a sense that Tolkien's artistry and faith have succeeded in
kindling and rekindling, resulting in his writing a story that enriches

primary creation. One of the ways in which he achieves this effolia-
tion of reality is by his situating the events of the trilogy within a secondary world that is true to its mythic self even as it conforms in all
important ways with the primary creation that provides the trilogy
with its rock and stone, water and air, earth and tree, men and other
reasoning beings.

He begins the trilogy with a Prologue that explains the background for the story and, in so doing, adds to the consistency of the
work:

> Further information will also be found in the selection
> from the Red Book of Westmarch that has already been
> published, under the title of *The Hobbit*. That story was
> derived from the earlier chapters of the Red Book, com-
> posed by Bilbo himself, the first Hobbit to become famous
> in the world at large, and called by him *There and Back
> Again*.[11]

This passage connects the trilogy with the earlier *Hobbit*, the book
that grew out of stories Tolkien told his children,[12] and to *The Red
Book*, a work that exists only in the world of the trilogy[13] (although
fragments and stories to which Tolkien alludes in the trilogy as part
of the lore of *The Red Book* have been published since his death[14]).
Nor is allusion to records and histories unique in this passage.[15] His
work is filled with poems that tell of events in a variety of pasts upon
which characters reflect. In one of the most moving passages in the
trilogy, Frodo, the hero, and his companion, the loyal Sam, are sitting exhausted, outside the tunnel through which they must travel to
continue their journey to the Cracks of Doom, the only place in
which the ring may be destroyed. Their conversation reveals just
what a tale means to them:

> "I don't like being here at all," said Frodo, "step or
> stone, breath or bone. Earth, air, and water all seem
> accursed. But so our path is laid."
> "Yes, that's so," said Sam. "And we shouldn't be here
> at all, if we'd known more about it before we started. But I
> suppose it's often that way. The brave things in the old tales
> and songs, Mr. Frodo: adventures, as I used to call them. I
> used to think that they were things the wonderful folk of the
> stories went out and looked for ... But that's not the way of
> it with the tales that really mattered, or the ones that stay in
> the mind. Folk seem to have been just landed in them, usu-

ally – their paths were laid that way …But I expect they had lots of chances, like us, of turning back, only they didn't. And if they did …they'd have been forgotten. We hear about those as just went on – and not all to a good end" (*TT* IV:8, 320–21).

These comments occur, of course, in this imagined narrative; at the same time, they have significance that transcends the imagined world. These characters are dealing with the most essential things that all men must confront: fate and free will, victory and defeat, virtue and vice. Moreover, the conversation serves to reinforce a fundamental theme in Tolkien's work: what is occurring is real and is part of a story and the story goes on.

In similar fashion, after the destruction of the ring, as Frodo and Sam await what seems to be sure death, Sam speaks:

What a tale we have been in … I wish I could hear it told? Do you think they'll say: *Now comes the story of Nine-fingered Frodo and the Ring of Doom*? And then everyone will hush, like we did, when in Rivendell they told us the tale of Beren One-hand and the Great Jewel. I wish I could hear it! And I wonder how it will go on after our part (*RK* VI:4, 228–29).

After their rescue and the beginning of their healing, the two are at a great banquet where they are honored:

And when the glad shout had swelled up and died away again, to Sam's final and complete satisfaction and pure joy, a minstrel of Gondor stood forth, and knelt, and begged leave to sing. And behold! He said:
"Lo! Listen to my lay. For I will sing to you of Frodo of the Nine Fingers and the Ring of Doom."
And when Sam heard that he laughed aloud for sheer delight, and he stood up and cried: "O great glory and splendour! And all my wishes have come true!" And then he wept (*RK* VI:4, 232).

Another scene that reinforces the truth of tales occurs as Frodo prepares for his final journey with those leaving Middle Earth now that the Third Age has ended. He gives Sam:

…a big book with plain red leather covers; its tall pages were now almost filled. At the beginning there were many

leaves covered with Bilbo's thin wavering hand, but most of it was written in Frodo's firm flowing script...
"Why you have nearly finished it, Mr. Frodo!," Sam exclaimed ... "I have quite finished, Sam," said Frodo. "The last pages are for you." (*RK* VI: 9, 307).

Borne out here is Tolkien's conviction that "there is no true end to any fairy-tale" (*Leaf* 68).

The stories in these passages are presented as if they were history, a record of human action, important because the actions of rational beings made in the image and likeness of God have eternal significance. This same sense of the high dignity of the person is behind Tolkien's careful attention to psychological verisimilitude. The devising of seeming truth is necessary because in a fantasy the writer must convince the reader that the secondary world with its characters who are unique to it are real. Tolkien adapts most of his characters from traditional lore, and he stays true to the mythic ethos that each has. Moreover, he creates his own mythic rational being:

In a hole in the ground there lived a hobbit. Not a nasty, dirty, wet hole, filled with the ends of worms and an oozy smell, not yet a dry, bare, sandy hole with nothing in it to sit down on to eat: it was a hobbit-hole, and that means comfort.[16]

In his description of Bilbo's home, Tolkien makes sure that the reader recognizes the uniqueness of this being, this Halfling (*The Hobbit*, 10). All who meet Hobbits, whether Wizards, Elves, Ents, Dwarves, Orcs, Men, Barrow-wights, Nazgul, even Sauron, are surprised by their valor. Gandalf says:

Hobbits really are amazing creatures, as I have said before. You can learn all that there is to know about their ways in a month, and yet after a hundred years they can still surprise you at a pinch (*FR* I:2, 72).

That many underestimate them because their love of comfort gives rise to one of the many themes of the novel: "It is shown that looks may belie the man – or the halfling" (*RK*, V:1, 28).

Other themes in the trilogy are informed by Tolkien's conviction that every part of creation is sacramental including his creation.[17] Thus, the themes that arise from the events of the novel are recognizably human. For example, Tolkien depicts the allure of evil even for those who would be virtuous. The halfling Bilbo, the eloquent and generous hero in *The Hobbit* ends, and a major figure as *The Fellowship of the Rings* begins; this reveals the influence that the central symbol of evil, the ring, has on him. When Gandalf the Wizard asks him if he intends to keep his promise to leave the ring to Frodo, Bilbo answers in an uncharacteristic manner:

> "Now it comes to it, I don't like parting with it at all, I may say. And I don't really see why I should. Why do you want me to?" he asked, and a curious change came over his voice. It was sharp with suspicion and annoyance. "You are always badgering me about my ring…"
>
> Bilbo flushed, and there was an angry look in his eyes. His kindly face grew hard… "It is my own, I found it. It came to me."
>
> "Yes, Yes," said Gandalf. "But there is no need to get angry."
>
> "If I am it is your fault," said Bilbo. "It is mine, I tell you. My own. My precious. Yes, my precious" (*FR* I:1, 42–43).

After further struggle with Gandalf, an externalization of his psychomachia, Bilbo surrenders the ring: "A spasm of anger passed swiftly over the hobbit's face again. Suddenly it gave way to a look of relief and a laugh" (*FR* I:1, 43). Here Tolkien gives a foreshadowing of what occurs in the climax of the trilogy when Frodo stands at the Crack of Doom: "'I have come,' he said. 'But I do not choose now to do what I came to do. I will not do this deed. The Ring is mine!'" (*RT* VI:3, 223). And just as Bilbo when he surrenders the ring is restored to himself, so too Frodo, once the ring is lost, is restored: "In his eyes there was peace now, neither strain of will, nor madness, nor any fear. His burden was taken away" (*RT* VI:3, 224).

In a letter written in 1963, Tolkien comments on the significance of Frodo's failure, saying that "it became quite clear that Frodo after all that had happened would be incapable of voluntarily destroying the Ring."[18] Tolkien says that "Frodo indeed 'failed' as a hero," but insists that this was not "a *moral* failure" because "Frodo had done what he could and spent himself completely (as an instrument of Providence) and had produced a situation in which the object of his quest could be achieved."[19] Frodo had begun this negative quest humbly: "I do really wish to destroy it …Or, well, to have it destroyed. I am not made for perilous quests. I wish I had never seen the Ring! Why did it come to me? Why was I chosen?" (*FR* I:2, 70). Because of this humility "and his sufferings ...[Frodo was] justly rewarded by the highest honour; and his exercise of patience and mercy towards Gollum gained him Mercy."[20] Not only do his comments to Sam as their terrible journey proceeds foreshadow his failure, they also reveal this humility and suffering:

> To *do the job* as you put it – What hope is there that we ever shall? And if we do, who knows what will come of that? If the One goes into the Fire, and we are at hand? I ask you, Sam, are we ever likely to need bread again? I think not. If we can nurse our limbs to bring us to Mount Doom, that is all we can do. [Even that is] more than I can, I begin to feel (*TT* IV:2, 231).

In the 1963 letter cited above, Tolkien adverts to two other themes: first, that behind all events there is a pattern and a maker of that pattern. Fourteen years after Bilbo's party and disappearance and nine years after his last visit, Gandalf reappears and tells Frodo what the significance and history of the ring are. After characterizing Bilbo's finding the ring as "the strangest event in the history of the Ring so far," Gandalf continues:

> "There was more than one power at work, Frodo. The Ring was trying to get back to its master....
> "Behind that there was something else at work, beyond any design of the Ring-maker. I can put it no plainer than by saying that Bilbo was *meant* to find the Ring, and *not* by its maker. In which case you also were *meant* to have it. And that may be an encouraging thought" (*FR* I:2, 65).

The second theme is that men are to be merciful to each other. Frodo's mercy enabled the destruction of the ring to occur even at the moment when it looked as if the negative quest had failed. But Frodo, before he undertakes his quest, does not feel mercy toward Gollum. When he hears the tale of his contest with Bilbo under the earth (*The Hobbit*, 79–100), Frodo says to Gandalf: "What a pity that Bilbo did not stab that vile creature, when he had the chance?... he is as bad as an Orc, and just an enemy. He deserves death." Gandalf's reply is one of the richest thematic passages in the trilogy:

> "Deserves it! I daresay he does. Many that live deserve death. And some that die deserve life. Can you give it to

them? Then do not be too eager to deal out death in judgment. For even the very wise cannot see all ends. I have not
much hope that Gollum can be cured before he dies, but
there is a chance of it. And he is bound up with the fate of
the Ring. My heart tells me that he has some part to play
yet, for good or ill, before the end; and when that comes the
pity of Bilbo may rule the fate of many—yours not least"
(*FR* I:2, 68–69).

Free will, consequences, sin, virtue, hope, and the wisdom of the
heart are the threads that constitute the thematic fabric of this passage. That Frodo has embraced Gandalf's wisdom because of his
suffering is apparent in the scene in which he finally meets Gollum
face to face. Frodo rescues Sam from Gollum's grasp by threatening
to cut his throat, and Gollum begs for his life. After Frodo recalls
Gandalf's earlier words, he says to Sam: "I am afraid [of Gollum's
villainy]. And yet, as you see, I will not touch the creature. For now
that I see him, I do pity him" (*TT* IV:1, 221–22). Later, this pity and
a sense of *comitatus* cause Frodo to save Gollum from a just death at
the hands of Faramir and his men, warrior-hunters. Frodo goes to the
forbidden pool to fetch Gollum, who thinks he is alone and does not
know that his being in this place is punishable by death:

> Frodo shivered, listening with pity and disgust. He
> wished it would stop, and that never need hear that voice
> again … He could creep back and ask … the huntsmen to
> shoot. They would probably get close enough, while
> Gollum was gorging … Only one true shot, and Frodo
> would be rid of the miserable voice forever. But no, Gollum
> had a claim on him now. The servant has a claim on the
> master for service, even service in fear … Frodo knew, too,
> somehow, quite clearly that Gandalf would not have wished
> it (*TT* IV:6, 296).

Moreover, after bringing Gollum to Faramir, Frodo saves
Gollum's life by taking Smeagol – Gollum – under his protection (*TT*
IV:6, 300).

In all of these events Tolkien carefully constructs the various figures in the trilogy so that their actions are consistent with their moral
character. This psychological verisimilitude adds to the sense of significance of the thousand plus pages of the trilogy. Verisimilitude is
also present in the kinds of languages that characters speak, their
names, and the places in which they live. Tolkien's appendices at the

end of *The Return of the King* also contribute to the sense of reality, dealing with many subjects including genealogy, etymology, and chronology. They contribute to the reality of the secondary world of Middle Earth by their prosaic quality. For example, in his appendix, "On Translation," Tolkien says:

> It seemed to me that to present all the names in their original forms would obscure an essential feature of the times as perceived by the Hobbits (whose point of view I was mainly concerned to preserve): the contrast between a wide-spread language, to them as ordinary and habitual as English is to us, and the living remains of far older and more revered tongues (*RK* Appendix F 412).

This passage is typical of the appendices in its scholarly scope, its assumed factualness, its focus on a linguistic issue that a reader interested in the period would want to have analyzed. It is a veritable *tour de force* in its assumption that in this trilogy is a secondary world that the sub-creator, the author, allows the reader to enter.

Verisimilitude in describing places has profound thematic significance in the trilogy. The readers accept the reality of the geography and see how the places in the trilogy are emblems of the morality of the beings who live within them. The ultimate sign of evil is Sauron's Mordor:

> Upon its outer marges ... Mordor was a dying land, but it was not yet dead. And here things still grew, harsh, twisted, bitter, struggling for life. In the glens of the Morgai on the other side of the valley low scrubby trees lurked and clung, coarse grey grass-tussocks fought with the stones, and withered mosses crawled on them; and everywhere great withering, tangled brambles sprawled. Some had long thorns, some hooked barbs that rent like knives. The sullen shrivelled leaves of a past year hung on them, grating and rattling in the sad air, but their maggot-ridden buds were only just opening. Flies, dun or grey, or black, marked like orcs with a red eye-shaped blotch, buzzed and stung; and above the briar-thickets clouds of hungry midges danced and reeled (*RK* VI:2, 198).

Anti-life and hate-filled, Mordor embodies the nature of the being who has shaped it, Sauron, the Shadow, the Dark Lord, who himself is bodiless except for his "piercing Eye" (*e.g., RK* VI:3,

220). Mordor is the outward sign of the inward gracelessness of its ruler and his subjects.

Two places that are clearly beautiful and express the goodness of those who live within them are the Hobbits' Shire and the Elves' Lorien. The Shire is a place with rows of pleasant hobbit-holes, gardens, inviting lakes, flowing rivers, avenues of trees, fertile farms, clean air, good rain, ample sun, cleansing snow. However, in *The Hobbit*, the reader is aware that it is not Eden. Thus, the dreadful reign of Sharkey – Saruman – is made possible by Hobbits who cooperate with evil, thinking that they can control it.[21] When the four Hobbits return from their adventures, they find it fouled. Frodo arrives at his former home Bag End to gardens full of weeds and built over, blocked light, "piles of refuse," a "scarred" door, and a "bell that would not ring ...The place stank and was full of filth and disorder: it did not appear to have been used for some time" (*RK* VI:8, 297). Frodo calls this pollution in the Shire, "Mordor ... Just one of its works" (297). After the evil forces are routed from the Shire, the Hobbits rebuild and replant. Sam carefully puts "saplings in all the places where specially beautiful or beloved trees had been destroyed, and he put a grain of the precious dust [that Galadriel had given him so many months before in the land of the Elves] in the soil at the root of each" (*RK* VI:9, 303). "Altogether [the year following] ...was a marvelous year" (RK VI:9, 303).

This marvel is clearly connected with the Elvish gift that Sam uses to benefit all in the Shire. For everything that is connected with the Elves is beautiful, and perhaps in no other creation of Tolkien's imagination is his sacramental vision more apparent. Lothlorien, the home of Queen Galadriel, is fair:

> Evil had been seen and heard there, sorrow had been known; the Elves feared and distrusted the world outside: wolves were howling on the wood's borders: but on the land of Lorien no shadow lay (*FR* II:6, 364).

It is a place of trees, flowers, green hillsides, blue sky, afternoon sun, stars, fragrance, a place in which:

> Frodo stood awhile still lost in wonder. It seemed to him that he had stepped through a high window that looked on a vanished world. A light was upon it for which his language had no name. All that he saw was shapely, but the shapes seemed at once a clear cut, as if they had been first

> conceived and drawn at the uncovering of his eyes, and
> ancient as if they had endured forever. He saw no colour but
> those he knew, gold and white and blue and green, but they
> were fresh and poignant, as if he had at that moment first
> perceived them and made for them names new and won-
> derful. In winter here no heart could murmur for summer or
> for spring. No blemish or sickness or deformity could be
> seen in anything that grew upon the earth. On the land of
> Lorien there was no stain (*FR* II:6, 365).

In this place the desires described by Tolkien in his discourse on fairy-stories come true. And yet, an elegiac tone moves through all of things Elvish. When the ring is destroyed, if it is destroyed, they must leave Middle Earth, a grievous leaving. Galadriel tells Frodo:

> The love of the Elves for their land and their works is
> deeper than the deeps of the Sea, and their regret is undying
> and cannot be wholly assuaged. Yet they will cast all away
> rather than submit to Sauron (*FR* II:7, 380).

Explicit here is the painful condition of fallen man: even when he creates a goodly place in this world that he loves, it will pass away. That it does in no way diminishes its importance nor significance. Rather, at the end the lesser yields to the greater. And at the end of the trilogy, Tolkien has Frodo tearfully leave the restored Shire: "I have been too deeply hurt, Sam. I tried to save the Shire, and it has been saved, but not for me" (*RK* VI:9, 309). He leaves with Elrond and Galadriel:

> ... for the Third Age was over, and the Days of the Rings
> were passed, and an end was come of the story and song of
> those times. With them went many Elves of the High
> Kindred who would no longer stay in Middle-Earth; filled
> with a sadness that was yet blessed and without bitterness
> (*RK* VI:9, 309).

After farewells to Sam and Merry and Pippin:

> ... the ship went out into the High Sea and passed into the
> West, until at last on a night of rain Frodo smelled a sweet
> fragrance on the air and heard the sound of singing that
> came over the water ...the grey rain-curtain turned all to sil-
> ver glass and was rolled back, and he beheld white shores
> and beyond them a far green country under a swift sunrise
> (*RK* VI:9, 310).

The natural and the homely, high gifts that Frodo so loved that he gave himself to save them, recall to man his roots in Eden even as they prefigure the ultimate gifts that Frodo experiences in his destination beyond Middle Earth. Tolkien embodies in his story a message of joy, of *evangelium*: that which is beautiful here is a foretaste, a sign, a sacramental of the ineffable that awaits those who serve. He achieves through his narrative what he contends at the conclusion of his essay "On Fairie-Stories":

> All tales may come true; and yet, at the last, redeemed, they may be as like and unlike the forms that we give them as Man, finally redeemed, will be like and unlike the fallen that we know (*Leaf*, 73).

Dr. C. N. Sue Abromaitis is a Professor of English at Loyola College in Maryland. She specializes in Restoration and 18th century English Literature and the impact of the penal laws in Restoration and 18th century England on Dryden and Pope (among others). She also concentrates on the works of C. S. Lewis and J. R. R. Tolkien in literature and on the Catholic imagination. In addition to papers delivered and published on C. S. Lewis and J. R. R. Tolkien, she has also published papers on Gerard Manley Hopkins, Madeleine L'Engle and Alexander Pope.

Dr. Abromaitis has a B.A. from the College of Notre Dame in Maryland and an M.A. and Ph.D. from the University of Maryland. She is currently a Lady and Vice-Chancellor of the Mid-Atlantic Lieutenancy of the Equestrian Knights of the Holy Sepulcher of Jerusalem, a member of the Executive Board and Trustee at Mount de Sales Academy, and Secretary for the University Faculty for Life. She is married to Michael Abromaitis.

Notes

1 Saint Thomas Aquinas, *Summa Theologica*, Q.84, Art. 7.

2 *Hollywood vs. America* (New York: HarperCollins Publishers, 1992).

3 J. R. R. Tolkien, *The Letters of...* Ed. Humphrey Carpenter (Boston: Houghton Mifflin and Company, 1981), 194. This is an excerpt from a draft of a reply to criticism of his work by Peter Hastings, the manager of the Newman Book-shop in Oxford, dated September, 1954 (187–88). Tolkien marked at the top of the draft "Not sent," and commented that: "It seemed to be taking myself too importantly." (196).

4 J. R. R. Tolkien, *Tree and Leaf* (London: George Allen & Unwin, Ltd., 1965), 47. All citations to the work in the text are from this source and

will be indicated by (*Tree* and page number). The essay was originally composed as an Andrew Lang Lecture and was in a shorter form delivered in the University of Saint Andrews in 1938. It was eventually published, with a little enlargement, as one of the items in *Essays presented to Charles Williams*, Oxford University Press, 1947, now out of print. "It is here reproduced with only a few minor alterations" (*Leaf* vii–viii).

5   *The Letters*, 196.

6   I am indebted to "Nature and Grace after the Baroque," a paper by Father Stephen M. Fields, S. J., for his clear elucidation of Pope John Paul II's assessment of the relationship between reason and faith, and the natural and the supernatural. Presented at the biennial Jesuit Conference on the thought of John Paul II, Xavier University, Cincinnati, August 2000, it will be published by Fordham University Press, edited by John J. Conley, S. J. and Joseph W. Koterski, S. J.

7   John Paul II, *Encyclical Letter Fides et Ratio: On the Relationship between Faith and Reason* (Boston: Pauline Books and Media, 1998) chap. II, section 17, p. 30.

8   *The Letters*, 8–10. Carpenter in a note explains that four friends while in King Edward's School, Birmingham, in 1911 "formed themselves into an unofficial and semi-secret society which they called 'the T. C. B. S,' initials standing for the 'Tea Club and Barrovian Society'…" (8). This letter is Tolkien's response to the news of the death of one of the group in World War I. All were in the service at the time.

9   *Ibid*, 9.

10 *Ibid*, 10.

11 J. R. R. Tolkien, *The Fellowship of the Ring* in *The Lord of the Rings*, 2nd Edition (Boston: Houghton Mifflin Company, 1965), 10. All citations to the trilogy are taken from this edition: *The Fellowship of the Ring – FR; The Two Towers – TT; The Return of the King – RK* with Book: chapter, page numbers.

12 Humphrey Carpenter, *Tolkien* (Boston: Houghton Mifflin Company, 1977), 176ff.

13 Carpenter describes the beginning of Tolkien's life-long absorption with languages: "His mother introduced him to the rudiments of Latin, and this delighted him. He was just as interested in the sounds and shapes of the words as in their meanings, and she began to realize that he had a special aptitude for language" (22). He later notes that "Tolkien did not see himself as an inventor of story but as a discoverer of legend. And this was really due to his private languages" (75). Tolkien created a language "influenced by Finnish … and the more he worked at it the more he felt that it needed a 'history' to support it" (75).

14 These inculde *The Silmarillion* (1977), *Unfinished Tales* (1980), *The Book of Lost Tales* (1984), and *The Lays of Beleriand* (1985), all published by Houghton Mifflin Company.

15 See, for example, *RK* VI: 7, 295.

16 J. R. R. Tolkien, *The Hobbit* (Boston: Houghton Mifflin Company, 1966), 9. First published in September 21, 1937.

17 In an unsent draft of September, 1954 (see note 3), Tolkien says: "The Tale is after all in the ultimate analysis a tale, a piece of literature, intended to have a literary effect, and not real history." He tells Hastings that: "We differ entirely about the nature of the relation of sub-creation to Creation. I should have said that liberation 'from the channels the creator is known to have used already' is the fundamental function of 'sub-creation,' a tribute to the infinity of His potential variety, one of the ways in which indeed it is exhibited ... I am not a metaphysician; but I should have thought it a curious metaphysic – there is not one but many, indeed potentially innumerable ones – that declared the channels known (in such a finite corner as we have any inkling of) to have been used, are the only possible ones, or efficacious, or possibly acceptable to and by Him!" (188–89).

18 *The Letters*, 326.

19 *Ibid.*

20 *Ibid.*

21 Frodo's comments about Lotho as the Hobbits "scour" the Shire reveal his understanding of how people (Hobbits, in this case) can be corrupted by thinking they cannot lose power as they do evil (*RK* VI:8, 297).

Chapter 5
Sacred Architecture and the Christian Imagination
Steven J. Schloeder

What Is Happening with Greeley's Catholic Imagination?

It seems that every age of Christian church building, except for the last half of the previous century, has sought in some way to engage the Christian imagination through some expression of the heavenly realities through building, furnishing, decorating, and embellishing with sacred art. Only recently have we discarded this traditional approach of considering the church building as a symbolic presentation of a transcendental mystery in favor of one that speaks rather to the immanent, the communitarian, the functional, or the subjectively expressionistic.

The question of religious imagination is, of course, a perennial issue. It has lately come to the fore with Andrew Greeley's recent book *The Catholic Imagination,* in which he gives a sociological explication of the manner in which the Catholic worldview, which he correctly identifies as "sacramental" – that is, "a revelation of the presence of God"[1] – helps create a particular consciousness that serves Catholics as they navigate the American social landscape.

Greeley makes it clear that his work is not *theological* – it is *sociological.* His stated purpose is to test sociological hypotheses concerning the Catholic perceptions of material reality and the transcendent human longings for beauty, happiness, fulfillment, community, salvation, political order, and such against established sociological data. Thus, while his work is interesting, and indeed his conclusions are supportive of my own views, I wish to take the topic to a whole different level of consideration.

Now as my talk is explicitly about the *Christian* imagination, not the *Catholic* imagination, I think I ought to clarify what I consider to be the difference. Greeley discusses the explicitly Catholic aspects of

Christian culture: instantiated in the devotional life of Catholic devotionals such as those concerning "Mary the mother of Jesus, angels and saints, souls in Purgatory, statues, stained glass windows, holy water, religious medals, candles," and the like.[2] These are engaged in our developed Catholic understandings of sacred places and sacred time; of sexuality and desire as a sacramental longing and partial fulfillment of our relationship with the Divine Groom; of maternal love as found in our Catholic understanding of Mary as our heavenly mother; of what the Catholic understanding of our participation in the Body of Christ means for us as Catholics; of finding identity through living in community; and of having a sense of a well ordered society because the Church herself is a well ordered society.

Greeley follows David Tracy in holding that there are essential differences between Catholic and Protestant religious imaginations: Catholics tend to posit the presence of God in the World, classical Protestants his absence; Catholics the nearness of God to his creation, Protestants the distance; Protestants emphasize the risk of superstition and idolatry, Catholics the dangers of a creation in which God is only marginally present.[3] Thus Tracy and Greeley argue for an explicitly Catholic imagination, and I can go a long way with them on this.

Anagogy

Indeed, I shall argue for a Catholic understanding of the relationship between the material world that we perceive, and the transcendent reality of the spiritual plane, not merely as analogy within our analogical imagination, to use David Tracy's term, but as *anagogy*— a Greek term meaning "leading upward"—as the basis of understanding the Catholic sacramental system and the participation of the human imagination in this system. As time does not allow a more elaborate discourse on this, let it suffice to note that anagogy is a contemplative mode of participating in the spiritual things through material things, such as God in the person of Jesus, or the objective participation in grace through the sacraments. This understanding is rooted in the dictates of the Incarnation: that Christ is the very image of God. (John 1:1, Col 1:15, 2 Cor 4:4): "He who has seen me has seen the Father!"

Thus, within the sacrament of baptism, for instance, there is an intrinsic connection between the symbol and the effect: as water washes us so we are cleansed of our sins; as we can drown in water so do we die with Christ; as we are born in water, so are we born anew in the Church; as water nourishes and allows plants to grow, so are we nourished by the Holy Spirit as neophytes by the waters of baptism.

To understand anagogy, we must recapture a sense of the classical or medieval sense of "symbol": this is indeed difficult for us as moderns who, while we might have a platonic intuition, don't necessarily think of things as manifestation of heavenly realities. Today we think of a symbol as "something that represents something else by association, resemblance or convention" (to give a dictionary definition). Yet for pre-Reformation and pre-Enlightenment thinking, "symbol"—in its root sense of "thrown together"—was of such a connection between the physical and the spiritual realities, that a symbol was "the only objectively valid definition of reality."[4]

Effectively, the ritual process is an anagogical movement: the only way we can even begin to wrap our heads around the glory of God, or the heavenly worship of the Trinity, or the ongoing redemptive act of the Son eternally offering Himself to the Father, is through a liturgical symbolic structure of place, time, ritual movement and prayer, vestment, artifacts, and gestures. It is an event in space and chronological time, yet it is ordered to lead us to a transcending experience of an eternal and heavenly reality. It does so, in fact, by being an actual participation in that spiritual event that is signified. This is the goal of anagogical contemplation, and is the manner by which the sacramental system helps us attain and participate in the life of grace.

And yet for the purpose of this paper, I still wish to use the term "Christian imagination" because, as I hold, the entire order of our being as Christians is "to see Christ in all things." I do so not only for ecumenical reasons, but that we might sharpen the focus of our imaginations as we consider the matter of sacred architecture in order to see how Christ might reveal himself in the liturgy and in our church buildings.

The question of imagination, and the possibility of re-synthesizing a robust imaginal tradition, seems particularly appropriate for our day and age, when we as a Church are beginning to re-examine the previous century's trajectory toward liturgical simplification, and the corresponding artistic and architectural expressions which tend toward spartan, purportedly "functional," and decidedly aniconic liturgical spaces. This trajectory, which has its genesis in the overall

Image 1: Corpus Christi, Aachen, by R. Schwarz, 1929

movement toward abstraction in art – via the impressionists, fauvists, deStijl, expressionists, and Cubists movements in early 20th century art and architecture, which have their roots in Theosophy, Anthroposophy, and Eastern religions – raises questions far beyond the scope of this paper regarding what might even constitute "religion" or "spirituality"; or how such constructs could be expressed artistically and architecturally in a post-Enlightenment mentality. Matters related to epistemology, development of consciousness theory, cultural anthropology, and semiotics – to name just a few disciplines – would have to be called upon, all the while, one hopes, avoiding the babble of postmodernism.

So this paper might be considered more of a prolegomenon to such investigations, towards a critical understanding of the deep symbolic structure that underpins Catholic architectural, artistic, and liturgical traditions – so as to lay a solid groundwork for the inevitable and always continuous adjustments made in the post-conciliar implementation of the Second Vatican Council.

Liturgical Symbolism and the Human Person

Such an investigation requires, in my estimation, two primary foci of interest: the first concerns a reappraisal of "sacramentality" that accounts for our contemporary understanding of the observable universe – respecting the advances of science that preclude us from holding ancient cosmologies for which so much of traditional religion sought to account; and, secondly, a re-examination of those constitutive elements of sacred architecture that allow us to enter into an experience of the numinous. Therefore, I shall, in the remainder of this paper, attempt to schematize for us the structure of sacramental symbolism; indicate how the human person interacts with symbolically mediated presentations of spiritual realities via the faculty of imagination; give a few examples of how in the history of Christianity the Church has sought to convey transcendent expressions through architectural forms; and, finally, conclude with some thoughts about what all this means practically for the future of sacred art, ecclesiastical architecture, and the Church's liturgical expression.

A Sacramental Cosmos

The ground of this inquiry must be creation – the order of being as we know and experience it. While this is, in a certain sense, pre-Revelational (that is, Revelation as God has chose to reveal himself to the human community through his Word and the Incarnation), it necessarily does presuppose another level of revelation: namely, that God has ordered the material world – in effect, created a *cosmos* out

Image 2: The Great Architect

of *chaos* – and has endowed humanity with both the ability and desire to know and love God through the material order. Thus, the idea of material order – that there is indeed an order to the material world by which we can search for and come to know the Orderer – is central to my thesis. These things must be axiomatic – not provable in a sense – that God has created the material world so as to mediate knowledge of himself to us, that he has created a symbolic universe, and that he has created the human person as a symbol knowing and symbol using being. As such, he has given us the tools – chiefly the senses, imagination, and intellect – to know him through mediating symbol structures.

It is my guess that this was not always necessarily so: that indeed Adam and Eve in some manner walked with God in the cool of the evening, and that in our original state of prelapsarian perfection, we required no mediation to know, love, and commune with God. To understand this, and to understand our present condition, let us briefly consider the question through the lens of Catholic anthropology.

We know that we are made body and soul: that the soul gives form to our body and makes us that which we are. That we have a human soul makes us human; that we have a unique and individual human soul makes us unique and individual human persons. Each soul is individual and unique in creation, and there is a complete and organic unity between the body and the soul in a living human person.

God gave us the two great faculties of the soul – will and intellect – that give us the capacity of thinking and acting. Our intellect is ordered toward knowing the truth, our will is ordered toward seeking the good. Since God is the source of all being – and all being is existentially good – and God is the creator of reality – and truth is a matter of correspondence with reality – we can say that these two great faculties are given us to know and desire God.

It is through the intellect that we make judgments as to the nature of reality: the object of the intellect is being itself: it is the true, and truth lies in making valid correspondences between what we think a thing is and what it actually is. Similarly, it is through the will that we move our being to possess that which is good. And yet all being is existentially good, but we cannot go around trying to acquire all goods for ourselves: for that would be chaos, and lead to injustice (for we would try to acquire goods that are not rightfully ours to take). And so it is given to our intellect to instruct our will as to the higher goods that should be pursued.

But the human person is more complex than just a soul with volition and intellection in a body. For we also have imagination and memory as two distinct operations of the soul, as well as senses through which we perceive the world; and we also have appetites and passions and emotions that mediate between the self and the world. The imagination, in the strict sense, is a storehouse of images (called phantasms), which are created from the sensory data taken in through our sense organs: eyes, ears, nose, taste buds, and skin. It is a synthetic faculty, allowing us to merge ideas and images, so as to allow both for analogous reasoning and for creativity. It is also the seat of our imaginal memory, so that we can remember the sound of our mother's voice, where we live, what spaghetti tastes like, and even what we look like when we see ourselves in a mirror.

Now for Adam and Eve, who walked with God in the Garden of Eden, in a state of original justice, all things worked properly: the senses received knowledge of being (say, of each other, or of God, or of an apple), and the intellect perfectly understood whatever the human being *could possibly* know of each other, God, or apples. Knowing a thing to be a good, the will was thus oriented to procuring the good for the good of the person. The appetites, passions, and emotions thus followed suite so that the entire person was unified in knowing, desiring, feeling, and sensing the good: whether it was God, each other, or an apple, there was an immediate and participatory relationship between the knower and the known. Importantly, this immediate and participatory knowing *is* a love relationship.

This is a very important point: in the garden – in our unfallen state – we knew things immediately: thus we knew them as they actually were, we were attracted to their intrinsic goodness, and we loved truly all things perfectly.

The serpent's great promise to Eve was: "For God knows that in the day you eat from it your eyes will be opened, and you will be like God, knowing good and evil." (Gen. 3:5). In this, he did not lie: the human race did indeed learn both good and evil, just like the gods. God, however, never intended that we should know of evil. Sadly for us, the human soul was not made to know evil, privation, or error: it was rather made to know only goodness: especially the *summum bonum* of God himself. Adam and Eve never did have the capacity to be able objectively *to evaluate* between good and evil, or between what is true and complete good from what is partial or defective good. This is why God originally gave us the ability to know things *connaturally*, to know things immediately and through direct participation: so that we would not need to know of privation, of partial goods, of goods known not in themselves but now in respect to one another.

Thus, humanity entered into its fallen state. Faced with the impossibility of perfectly knowing and choosing between multiple goods, the intellect clouded by the knowledge of evil it was never intended to have, and the will weakened by the pull of differing and conflicting goods, the will and intellect no longer were able to work harmoniously. Mankind was thus necessarily separated from God because now we could no longer know Him *as He is* but only in reference to other things. We could no longer walk with God in the cool of the evening; we could no longer know contingent being – the animals and the plants – connaturally. We were thus thrust into a hostile relationship with God himself, and with all of his creation, including ourselves. Thus did God command that we toil for our living; that nature would no longer cooperate with us; that there would be a tension between man and woman; and that we would be banished from the garden so as not to attempt to acquire immortality by eating of the other tree of life.

After the fall, whatever that really means, God in his Providence did not abandon us to a fate of never knowing him. In our present human condition, when we no longer know immediately, we know chiefly by sense impression. And yet we can still know quite a bit through this: in fact, St. Paul tells us in Rom 1:19–20 that we can even know of God by what He has created:

> For what can be known about God is plain to them, because God has shown it to them. Ever since the creation of the world his invisible nature, namely, his eternal power and deity, has been clearly perceived in the things that have been made.

And yet, since we can no longer know immediately the essence of particular things, or of persons, we must content ourselves to know by those material conditions that present themselves to our sense faculties: things we see, hear, touch, taste, and smell. So how then do we know things that are beyond the grasp of our senses: the spiritual realities?

Well, of course we certainly do know by revelation and faith, but I would suggest that we are meant in our fallen condition to know of God primarily through symbol. And I believe this is God's plan, ameliorating as much as possible the epistemological disaster of the Fall from grace. Now it is quite a statement to say that we *can*, let alone *do*, know God, and the things of God, primarily through symbol. In answer to such an objection, Dorothy L. Sayers wrote:

> All language about God must, as St Thomas Aquinas pointed out, necessarily be analogical. We need not be surprised at this, still less suppose that because it is analogical it is therefore valueless or without any relation to the truth. The fact is that all language about everything is analogical; we think in a series of metaphors. We can explain nothing in terms of itself, but only in terms of others things...In particular, when we speak about something of which we have no direct experience, we must think by analogy or refrain from thought. It may be perilous, as it must be inadequate, to interpret God by analogy with ourselves, but we are compelled to do so; we have no other means of interpreting anything."[5]

Now it seems, after years of the Cartesian reductionism and impoverished anthropology which have affected our epistemological discussions, we are again coming to understand the power of symbol as a primary way of knowing – let alone of engaging the religious imagination. Andrew Greeley notes that: "Cognitive psychologists have recently begun to insist that metaphors – statements that one reality is like another reality – are the fundamental tools of human knowledge. We understand better and explain more adequately one reality to ourselves by comparing it to another reality which we already know."[6] And so, if this was indeed God's plan, He began to reveal himself through symbols.

In Genesis and Exodus, God appears as a smoking brazier and a flaming torch (Gen 15:7–18); as an angel (Gen: 16: 7–13); as the three visitors (Gen. 18); as a burning bush (Ex 3); as a column of cloud by day and a pillar of fire by night (Ex 13:21–22); in fire on Mount Sinai (Ex 19:18); and He orders the ark and the tabernacle enclosure constructed to localize his symbolic presence among the Israelites (Ex 25:8). In Exodus we read: "They shall make a sanctuary for me, that I may dwell in their midst. This Dwelling and all its furnishings you shall make exactly according to the pattern that I will now show you."

God made it perfectly clear that the spiritual world can be symbolized through material things, for He ordered them to make two cherubim of gold on each side of the ark (Ex 25:18), and to embroider the tent covering with cherubim (Ex 26: 1).

Thus, we have a very clear sense in the Old Testament of a symbolic connection with the spiritual world. And, of course, in the fullness of time, God showed himself as man, in the person of Jesus Christ: a man to be understood as a man, and yet not limited to being a man.

This is important for understanding symbolism: we must be able to grasp the thing in itself – Jesus as man, or water as cleansing, or water as something dangerous and deadly – in order for us to grasp the thing it symbolizes. The reality symbolized will always be incomparably more than the symbol. If it were not so, a symbol would be a mere sign: *this* means *that*; or it would be simple algebra: $X = Y$. Rather, symbols will be multivalent, layered, sometimes clear and sometimes obscure, complex, and non-linear. After all, a symbol is trying to communicate something that words cannot. The image of Christ on the cross can express far more than all the books ever written about the topic.

The Symbolic Nature of Church Architecture

Having looked at both the human person's symbolic mode of knowing, and of the specific question of anagogy, I wish now to summarize briefly the main themes that run through the Christian building tradition.

There are three major themes in Christian architecture: the *temple* (and its antecedent, the tabernacle), the *city*, and the *body* (as well as innumerable minor themes). These themes, rooted in scriptural revelation, are still upheld as the primary archetypes in the documents of the Second Vatican Council,[7] in the rite of *Dedication of a Church and Altar*,[8] and in the universal *Catechism*.[9] They all, I would suggest, offer the possibility for understanding anagogically the order of Christ's Church because they each explain the Kingdom of God as "parts to the whole," where each part has its own necessary function, form, location, and symbolic meaning; and where the whole has its own sense of organic completion and perfection in which the whole is greater than the sum of the parts.

Most significantly, these three terms come together in Revelation 22, wherein the "Holy City, the new Jerusalem, coming down out of heaven from God" is called "the dwelling of God with man" (the Latin here is *Dei tabernaculum cum hominibus*, recalling the desert tabernacle); and this tabernacle is concretized as the Temple, which is the person of Jesus as the Lamb, thus invoking the Body as well: "And I saw no temple in the city, for its temple is the Lord God the Almighty and the Lamb."

So, as we have seen with symbol structure in general, the complexity and multivalency, and even ambiguity, of these terms create a richer fabric for our contemplation, allowing us to enter into the spiritual reality in a nonlinear, poetic, and intuitive mode. Let us consider these three forms more in detail:

Temple

The temple form is a rich theme, rooted in the Egyptian temples built by Ramses II, the Pharaoh from whom Moses delivered the Israelites. Once delivered, this temple form took on a transitory, tent-like nature in the desert tabernacle. The fabrication and arrangement

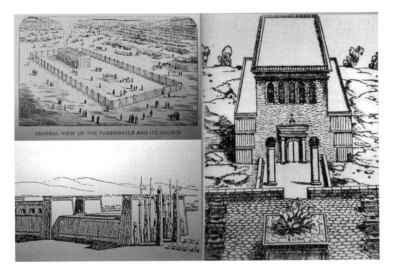

Image 3: Three Phases of the Temple

of the desert tabernacle, wherein God dwelt in the midst of the Twelve Tribes, was carefully specified to Moses by the Lord in the book of Exodus: the tent itself and all its furnishing, the altar of holocaust, the court of dwelling, the lavabo, the table of shewbread, and so forth. This arrangement has set the course for churches, and the idea of the *tabernacle* – from *taverna*, the Greek word for "tent" – is often found stylized in the baldacchino over the altar.

In the book of Kings, Solomon is commissioned by God to design a temple, which is effectively a re-concretization of the transient desert tabernacle. The arrangement of the priestly courtyard with altar and lavabo, and the temple proper with its sanctuary and the Holy of Holies, separated by the veil, follows the same form as the ancient desert dwelling. One can notice the influence of Egyptian temple architecture in the Jerusalem temple, even down to the pillar-like forms of Jakin and Boaz at the entry.

In the New Testament, the temple becomes a metaphor to describe the Church, even as Christ likened his own body to the temple. In this Great Building, St. Mark calls Jesus the cornerstone (Mk 12:11), St. Luke in Acts calls him the keystone (Acts 4:8), St. Paul, the foundation (1 Cor 3:11), and St. John, the door (Jn 10:9).

In the Greco-Roman tradition of temple architecture, there are anthropomorphic expressions of mythical and hieratic elements, where the column with its base, shaft, and capital is likened to a human body with its feet, trunk, and head. Thus we can see how Scripture can call the apostles "columns" which support the building (Saint Paul calls James, Cephas and John "pillars" in Gal 2:9), and the people are the actual "living stones...built into a spiritual house" (1 *Pet* 2:4). Ephesians 2:19–22 compares the whole Church to the house of God: Christ is the Cornerstone, the apostles and prophets are the foundations, and the Lord joins together the people to form a holy temple that becomes "a dwelling place of God in the Spirit."

Throughout the Patristic and Middle Ages, the idea of the temple as a great building was allegorically developed in both the East and West in the writings of Eusebius,[10] the Venerable Bede,[11] St. Maximus the Confessor,[12] St. Germanos,[13] Hugh of St.-Victor,[14] and William Durandus.[15] Such anagogical literature, where church buildings and the parts of the holy liturgy were explained in terms of the historical, allegorical, moral, and spiritual lessons they held for us, continued to influence architects in the Renaissance and Baroque

Image 4: Anthropomorphic architecture

ages, as evidenced in the works of Borromini and Guarini, and were revived in the 19th Century, especially among the Anglicans, through the scholarship of the Cambridge Camden Society and the Alcuin Club.

The idea of the Church as Temple found particular expression in Renaissance and Baroque ages, when the invention of archeology as a science gave the Renaissance architects a ready architectural vocabulary of Greco-Roman forms upon which to build a theory of temple architecture. That said, the themes of the Church as temple are already well established in the Byzantine age – Hagia Sophia was justly compared to the glory of Solomon's Temple, and Justinian was recorded as saying, "Solomon, I have surpassed thee!" In the middle ages, Jean Fouquet had no hesitation of portraying Solomon's Temple in the guise of a Gothic cathedral.

Throughout the Renaissance, the idea of the Temple inflamed the Christian imagination: it was however, more the patrimony of Solomon's Temple, rather than the Greco-Roman orders *per se* that underpinned this tradition. This is most clearly evidenced in the work of the 16th and 17th century Spanish Jesuits who worked on hypothetical reconstructions of the Temple of Solomon and the Temple of Ezekiel.[16] Among these reconstructions, they developed the theory of the Solomonic Order, best known from Bernini's massive baldacchino in St. Peter's, as the primordial order – the "revealed" order from which all the other Greco-Roman orders derived. Here at St. Peter's we see can see the original Constantinian columns from the 4th century tomb of the Apostle now set into niches. The Solomonic order was readily identified with the temple of Solomon, as seen in this medieval depiction by Fouquet. Thus there is a connection uniting the Christian architectural tradition with the Temple of Solomon. Other evocations of the Temple of Solomon are the two exterior columns, Jakin and Boaz, that we read of in the Book of Kings. This symbol is writ large in Fischer von Erlach's *Karlskirche* in Vienna, where the Jakin and Boaz columns are conflated with Trajan's column to express the connection of this church with the perfection of the Temple in the Victory of Christ.

City

The city of Jerusalem certainly has mythic power, and so both the physical city on Mount Moriah and its anagogic reality as the Heavenly Jerusalem have long held the imagination of theologians and architects. The Church, when cast in the language of urban planning, is ecclesiologically expressed in another complex analogy of part to the whole. St. John writes that the apostles are foundations that support the walls around of the City of God (Rev 21:14); while St Paul sees the believers are individual temples of the Holy Spirit in the City of God (1 Cor 3:16–17, 6:19; 2 Cor 6:16). St. John's imagery of the heavenly Jerusalem inspired church builders in the mid-Patristic period: San Stefano Rotondo is a 5th century stylization of the Celestial City. Note the similarity with the arrangement of the Desert Tabernacle.[17] The early Christian basilica, such as old St. Peter's at the Vatican, and the later medieval monastery, were each ordered as virtual cities unto themselves, with gates, plazas, circulation routes, arranged complexes of buildings zoned for their functions and "civic" presence.

For the medievals, the analogical symbolism was an organic reality. A city, like a human body, like a building, is an assemblage of individual components, each with a form and location determined by its function or purpose. Whether speaking in terms of limbs and organs in the body, or of city walls, gates, roads, piazzas, and various kinds of buildings in the city, the church building with its various functions was readily likened to these archetypes. Summerson's reading of the Gothic cathedral as a vast city comprised of shrines, aedicules, tombs, altars, and chantry chapels, with the ambulatory as a great circulation routes, is particularly persuasive.[18]

It is also clear that for these medieval builders, their churches were deliberate evocations of the City of God. In 1135, Abbot Suger of St. Denis commenced the rebuilding of the old Romanesque basilica into what is universally considered the first Gothic church. Soaring and radiant, elegant, articulated, ornamented, gilded, and

Image 5: Church as *Civitas Dei*

refined, this abbey church was in the mind of Suger a representation of the Heavenly City, the New Jerusalem, that "city of pure gold, crystal clear…that needed neither sun nor moon, for the glory of God gave it light, and its lamp was the Lamb" (Rev 21:18 and 23). Suger sought to make his new church a complete participation in the heavenly Jerusalem, and his accounting of the design and construction of St.-Denis is an important text in understanding the medieval understanding of anagogy.[19]

Body

No more clearly can this concept of part to the whole be seen than in understanding the church as a body. Certainly the body is one of the earliest symbols known to humanity. The primal symbol is the woman's body: the mother, with all her mystery of fertility, fecundity, and nourishment. Thus the chthonic religions met in caves, entering into the womb of the Great Earth Mother. Among the earliest of known ritual architecture are the 7000-year-old Hypogea in Malta. The form of the woman, fertile with broad hips and nourishing with large breasts, seems to be symbolically expressed in the arrangement of the interior spaces of these earliest of temples.[20]

Image 6: Church as Body

The Egyptian temple, as well, seems to be cosmologically ordered to the proportions of the human person, as Schwaller de Lubicz demonstrates.[21]

So it was not new when St. Paul used the metaphor of the body to create an analogy between the visible Church and the mystical Body of Christ (cf. Rom 12:4–5 and 1 *Cor* 12:12–26). With this understanding, by the year 380 A.D., Saint Ambrose intentionally ordered constructed a church in a cruciform to symbolize the Victory of Christ. For the medievals, the apse at the head of the church spoke to the seat of governance where the bishop sat; the crossing was the chest where the altar was placed at the heart of the church; the arms were the transepts, derived from the bema, where the deacons and sub orders were placed to assist the priests; and the body of the church was where Christ's lay faithful, his embodied presence on earth participated in the liturgy.

But we ought ask, in what manner does the body represent the church? Here we must speak of the "analogy of the body": we can create an analogy with the body primarily from our experience of our own bodies. Our body is an organic whole, a unity, comprised of separate but inseparable parts: the eye, the heart, the spleen, the neck, and the hand. Each part has its own function, its own form, its own particular location. To many parts we also ascribe poetic or symbolic meaning. Consider, for a moment, your own hand:

Form: It has a broad palm, hinged digits with an opposable thumb, and it has many and delicate nerve endings.

Function: because of its shape, it allows us to grasp things; because of its nerve structure it is a very sensitive sense organ, though which we can sense temperature, texture, moisture, and pressure. It can be closed to form a compact unit for striking, opened for receiving, and the fingers work independently for pointing, scratching, or other manual work.

Location: It is located on the end of the arm to maximize reaching.

Meaning: We ascribe also sorts of language to the hand: a "hand out," "crossing the palm with silver," "helping hands," "the finger of fate," and so forth. What we do with our hands has meaning: whether we shake hands in friendship or wag our finger at someone, whether we wring our hands in worry, or make a fist. We can slap, stroke, caress, poke, scratch, tickle with our hands, each indicating a different intentionality.

Likewise for the rest of the body: we speak of "putting your neck on the line," "sticking your nose in some one else's business," "having spleen," a "knee jerk" reaction, "giving someone the evil eye," or someone being "a pain in the rear." Thus the body has a poetry about it, which is intrinsically tied into the function, form, and location of the parts.

In church architecture, this four-fold understanding is conveyed by analogy. Let us look, for example, at an early Christian basilica.

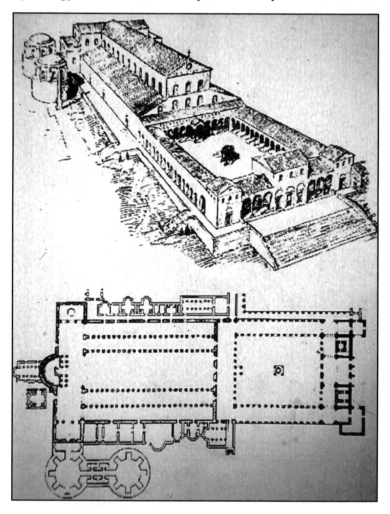

Image 7: Old Saint Peter's. Vatican City

As we have seen by the analogy of the city at old St. Peter's in the Vatican, so we can read the building much as we read our own bodies: there are intrinsic relationships between the form, the functions, the locations, and the meanings. We can begin to read from the outside the inside, so that the plan and the perspective readily read as integrated.

There is an open forecourt defined by various administration and residential buildings, a taller central nave with lower side aisles, a campanile, if we walked around the back we would see a pronounced apse declaring the chancel. Each part has its own function, form, location, and meaning: and we can discriminate between a baptistery, a sanctuary, a nave, a tomb, a side chapel, a sacristy, a bell tower, and so forth.

It is my contention that this analogy of the body is the underpinning structure of all traditional Catholic building, and it matters not whether it is rendered in Byzantine or Baroque, Romanesque or Revival, Medieval or Modern style. We have only recently lost this analogous understanding due to the explicit agenda of the early modernists that called for "universal space," which was defined only by the rearrangement of the furniture. The loss of this symbolic language, I suspect, is why people do not think of modern Catholic churches as "looking like churches"; but it is also my belief that we can discover a higher synthesis between this formal language and modern materials and building techniques.

Conclusion

These three great ideas, the Body of Christ, the Temple of the Holy Spirit, and the Celestial City, all spoke of the integrity and completeness of the Divine Order which buildings built for the Divine Liturgy ought to reflect. Across Christian history, each epoch of Christian building has sought to incarnate in its churches some architectural expression of the three great scriptural themes: the Body of Christ, the Temple of the Holy Spirit, and the Heavenly Jerusalem.

Today, I would suggest that in order to re-engage the Christian imagination, we again need to visit these great archetypes of church building, finding ways to express anew these ancient and revered models in materials, constructional methods, and with aesthetic sensibilities common to our present age. For what constitutes great church architecture is not a stylistic question, as if we only need

Image 8: St. Therese, Collinsville, Oklahoma, by S. Schloeder, 2000

again to build in Byzantine, Baroque, Romanesque, or Renaissance styles in order to have churches that are beautiful, meaningful, and appropriate. It is not a stylistic question, but a theological one; and the great Christian tradition is to engage the person in spiritual participation through material means: the anagogic basis of the sacraments, especially the holy liturgy, and the symbolic language of sacred art and architecture.

Stephen J. Schloeder is a registered architect in the states of Arizona and Oklahoma, specializing in the theory and design of

Catholic Church architecture. He graduated *cum laude* from Arizona State University with a B.A. in Architecture. He took an M.A. in Architecture from the University of Bath in 1989. In addition to his recent book, *Architecture in Communion*, he has published in *Crisis, Catholic World Report, Intercollegiate Review, Nexus,* and *University Bookman*. He is currently a doctoral candidate in Theology at the Graduate Theological Union in Berkeley, California.

Notes

1 Greeley, Andrew. *The Catholic Imagination*. Berkeley, 2000, p. 1.

2 *Ibid*, p. 5.

3 *Ibid*, p. 5.

4 von Simson, Otto. *The Gothic Cathedral*. New York, 1962, p. xix.

5 Sayers, Dorothy. *The Mind of the Maker*, London, 1941. pp 17–18.

6 Greeley, p. 6.

7 Vatican Council II, *Lumen Gentium*, 21 November 1964. Chap.1: 6 and 7.

8 Cf. Sacred Congregation for the Sacraments and Divine Worship. *Dedication of a Church and an Altar*. 29 May 1977.

9 *Catechism of the Catholic Church*. Washington DC, 1994. Cf. 753–757; 787–795; and 797–798.

10 Eusebius, *History of the Church*. Book 10, Chap. 4:67ff. Trans by G.A. Williamson. New York, 1965.

11 Bede. *On the Tabernacle*. Trans. by Arthur G. Holder. Liverpool UK 1994.

12 St. Maximus the Confessor, *Mystagogia*. PG 91:657 ff.

13 St. Germanos. *Church History*, PG 98: 384 ff.

14 Hugh of St.-Victor. *The Mystical Mirror of the Church*. Trans. by John Mason Neale and Benjamin Webb, in *The Symbolism of Churches*, London, 1893.

15 William Durandus. *De Rationale Divinorum Officiorum*. Trans. by John Mason Neale and Benjamin Webb, in *The Symbolism of Churches*, London, 1893.

16 Cf. Rykwert, Joseph. *On Adam's House in Paradise*. New York, 1972.

17 Ritz S.J. Sandor. *L'Insuperabile Creazione del Passato, Presente e Futuro; Il Tempio Perenne di Santo Stefano Rotondo in Roma; La Nuova Gerusalemme dell' Apocalisse* (Rome: Edizione speciale riservata all'autore, undated).

18 Cf. Summerson, Sir John. *Heavenly Mansions*. New York 1963.

19 Cf. Panofsky, Erwin. *Abbot Suger: On the Abbey Church of St.-Denis and its Art Treasures*. 2nd Edition. Princeton, 1979.

20 Cf. Eliade, Mircea. *The Forge and the Crucible*. New York, 1971.

21 Schwaller De Lubicz, R. A. *The Temple in Man: Ancient Egyptian Sacred Architecture and the Perfect Man*, New York, 1988; also *The Temple of Man: The Apet of the South at Luxor*, New York, 1998.

Chapter 6
Response to Steven J. Schloeder's Paper on "Sacred Architecture and the Christian Imagination"
Catherine Brown Tkacz

To hear articulated the need for church architecture to be conceived on the basis of Catholic anthropology is refreshing, and Steven J. Schloeder expresses that anthropology fitly, demonstrating it from biblical, patristic, medieval, and modern texts. The first foundation for a church building must be conceptual, and Catholics in America have need for this to be understood by architects, to supplement and even to select from the guidelines found in the document issued by The National Conference of Catholic Bishops last November, *Built of Living Stones: Art, Architecture, and Worship*, itself intended to correct their problematic 1978 document, *Environment and Art in Catholic Worship*.[1] Our speaker today offered a salutary critique of the early draft of *Built of Living Stones* last year.[2] "That the World May Believe," the motto of this Fellowship, grounds my response to Mr. Schloeder's presentation, in both the pastoral and evangelical senses: the pastoral here being to teach doctrine to neophytes and to reinforce and to enrich that teaching for believers, and the evangelical being to make the authentic truth accessible to those who are not Catholic.

The "Christian imagination," he suggested, is the proper context for his presentation. The phrase is useful in two contexts, even essential in the second. First, "Christian imagination" refers without anachronism to the imagination of the faithful in the patristic and medieval eras who thought of themselves as *Christiani* in the time before "Catholic" and "Orthodox" could refer to subdivisions of the faithful, and, especially, before Protestantism; and this is the main sense in which Mr. Schloeder uses the phrase. Second, "Christian imagination" can focus on what is common to all Christians. In discussing Catholic church architecture, "Catholic imagination" is the fitting term. The Catholic imagination is informed by a particular belief in the nature and expressions of grace that is no longer common to all Christians. Focal in this understanding of grace are the sacraments, "the signs and instruments by which the Holy Spirit spreads the grace of Christ."[3] Not all Christians believe there are sacraments; Catholics do, and Catholic churches constitute the primary setting in which God gives grace to his people through those sacraments. Where there is a minister but not a priest, where there is an honored symbol of grape juice and bread but not the Mystery of the Holy Eucharist, there is no need for a sanctuary, for a specifically holy site; a "stage" may function better. Where a priest leads the people, and where Christ himself is present in the sacrament, let there be a sanctuary.

Regarding the conceptual foundation Mr. Schloeder has presented this morning, one welcomes his distinguishing between the *sacramental* understanding of reality, characteristic of the Catholic and Orthodox faithful, and the contrasting Protestant withdrawal from that. Mr. Schloeder makes this point most directly when speaking of anagogy, of how God draws us through the material to the spiritual. As he observes, the Incarnation brought about a "renewed, or perhaps new, relationship between the spiritual and the material." Further, one may add that the Catholic and Orthodox understanding of grace is that God truly can, and wills to, transform his faithful and to perfect them, not just nominally, but in substance; really and personally. The experience of God's transforming grace can baptize the intellectual capacity to create artistic expressions of reality; such a "sacramental imagination" effoliates, and effloresces, from faith in the sacraments and is rooted in the grace of God.

With Luther and Calvin and their adherents began an erosion of faith in grace as transforming, and thus a diminution of faith in the sacraments as efficacious for hallowing, and with this in turn came a profound distrust of the sacramental imagination. Ultimately, Protestant iconoclasm expresses disbelief that man, by grace, can become afresh His image, a living icon of God. It is no accident that during the iconoclasm of the 1560s in the Lowlands, often the church furnishings Catholics built to replace demolished ones again expressed typology that is both prophetic and sacramental, a typology that originally foretold the actions of the Messiah and that now also expresses the human capacity, by the grace of God, through a sacramental life to share in the experiences of Christ.

A case in point is the massive alabaster rood screen (15 m. x 7 m.) built in 1570–73 in the Cathèdrale de Notre Dame in Tournai, for it presents six depictions of events from Christ's passion, each above a depiction of an Old Testament type of that event, so that the faithful once again see the scourging of Christ prefigured by the martyrdom of the Maccabee brothers; Christ before Pilate prefigured by Susanna at her trial; Christ carrying the Cross prefigured by Isaac carrying the wood of his sacrifice; Christ on the Cross prefigured by the serpent lifted up in the wilderness; the Entombment of Christ prefigured by Jonah being swallowed by the whale; and Christ resurrecting and ascending prefigured by Jonah emerging from the whale.[4]

Church furniture, and architecture itself, can thus be pastoral and evangelical, can reinforce the truths already believed by the church community and visibly express them to those who could yet be more fully part of it. Catholic Church architecture – and its decoration and furnishings, and the art within it – needs, then, to be significantly different from Protestant models, on precisely the theological basis that Mr. Schloeder adduces.

The triad – fit number! – of major themes he identifies as traditionally informing the structure of the church building are the Temple, the City, and the Body. These themes are apt partly because they are also richly evocative of Heaven, in classical, Jewish and Christian thought, as Jeffrey Burton Russell has beautifully set forth in *A History of Heaven: The Singing Silence*.[5] Of the three symbols, temple, city, and body, primacy is claimed by Mr. Schloeder for the body as "the underpinning structure of all traditional Catholic building ... whether ... in Byzantine or Baroque, Romanesque or Revival, Medieval or Modern style." But Mr. Schloeder's emphasis on the metaphor of the body, on the evidence given, is overstated. He has shown that Ambrose and others designed church buildings to represent the cross and the proportions of the human body. The analysis by form, function, location, and meaning, that Mr. Schloeder offers for the body and for the church building, however, could be performed for any structure, not just body and church, but temple and city, and myriad other structures irrelevant to church architecture, such as a tree or a groundhog or a galaxy.

The dominant analogy may instead be the Temple with its interior Holy of Holies. As a Byzantine Catholic, who at Divine Liturgy faces the iconstasis, through the royal doors of which the priest comes out like Christ bringing the Eucharist to the faithful, I find the Temple dominant architecturally, especially the heart of the Temple, the Sanctuary. Historically, this seems to have been the case for Roman Catholic architecture as well. Only in modern architecture, in which the iconstasis shrank to a balustrade and then disappeared, is the architectural continuity with the Temple diminished. Traditionally, then, the paradigm of the Temple may be as important, or more important, than that of the body for Catholic church architecture.

And, at the start of the twenty-first century a further argument, one both pastoral and evangelical, can be made for choosing to continue and to revitalize the formal reference of Catholic architecture to the Temple through the structure of the Catholic sanctuary. Pastorally, such patterning can help express the coherence of revelation by physically recalling Christianity's Jewish beginnings and Christ's transformation of the Jewish inheritance by his sacrifice, which opened the sanctuary. The evangelical argument here draws on the image of the Body. For the Body of Christ includes "the righteous of all nations in every age," as Our Holy Father expressed it in the prayer for the Jubilee Year. The righteous Jews of the Old Testament, for instance, are of the Body of Christ. Thus did St. Augustine preach that the Maccabee brothers (feast day August 1) were "martyrs of Christ" who had confessed him in secret.[6] For contemporary church buildings to symbolize this belief by honoring the distinctness of the sanctuary bespeaks community with the others who believe in the One Creator God of Abraham, Isaac, and Jacob. Just so, a church building's geographic orientation continues to align worshiping Catholics, literally, with all persons who face East when they worship the One True God.

While identifying prime symbols, it is well to be explicit about what to avoid. Two pervasive American models are familiar and alluring, yet false. Mr. Schloeder's primary model, the analogy of the body, serves well here to critique the American models. First is the egalitarian, democratic model of the town hall, which favors the banal "barn-like" structure of the auditorium, which Mr. Schloeder has elsewhere justly criticized and shown to be in essence different from the similarly compact spaces of the cross and dome structure, as found in Hagia Sophia.[7] In the egalitarian American model, strongly influenced by Protestant thought, space is undifferentiated and designed to give everyone equal and immediate access to the sanctuary. This physically expresses the trend that, increasingly, human roles in the Church are undifferentiated, and the differences of gift and of vocation are downplayed as undemocratic embarrassments. But the egalitarian model here vitiates the image of the church as Body of Christ: it is as if everyone were the same part. Irresistibly, one imagines (perhaps not sacramentally) an unreflective liturgy planner asserting, "We are all elbows in the eyes of God." The other American model is fast food restaurants. If the functional model determining the structure of a church is efficient delivery of the Eucharist, the model is dysfunctional for worship. Jesus deserves better, and so do his people.

Most provocative in Mr. Schloeder's presentation is his insight that contemporary Catholic church architecture need not directly reproduce successful structures from the past. He is right, and this is unnerving, for we have all seen the merely new in architecture. To re-engage, to re-synthesize Catholic anthropology, architectural traditions, and new architectural possibilities, is a task needing the inspiration and wisdom and faith and learning that it has always needed. The baldachino over the altar can be an eloquent architectural symbol for the idea of the tablernacle as tent, but when this structural feature was introduced, it was stunningly new. What is needed now is innovation that is not merely stunning, or numbing, but truly a re-synthesis, or restatement. Mr. Schloeder's own design of the Church of St. Theresa, north of Tulsa, Oklahoma, with its affinities to San Vitale at Ravenna shows that old, even ancient models can be revisited effectively.

One could wish that all church architects were theologians and architectural historians, well versed in "a wider tradition of anagogical literature found in both east and west, where church buildings and the parts of the holy Liturgy were explained in terms of the historical, allegorical, moral, and spiritual lessons they held for us." An implication to be drawn from Mr. Schloeder's presentation is that once again the Church needs preachers and Catholic writers, clerical and lay, who can articulate the consonance between the church structure and the liturgy, so that new truly Catholic churches can be built; and so that the priests who will celebrate Mass within them can use them, in sermons and catechesis, as the inhabited visual aids they are meant to be – the better to teach the Body of Christ, "that the world may believe"!

Catherine Brown Tkacz holds a Ph.D. in Medieval Studies from the University of Notre Dame, (1983). She was the managing editor of the *Oxford Dictionary of Byzantium,* and has published numerous articles in such journals as *Studia Patristica, Vigiliae Christianae, Studies in Iconography, Revue des études augustiniennes,* and *Traditio,* in addition to articles in the *Intercollegiate Review.* She has given guest lectures at the Catholic University of America, Gonzaga University, and the University of Mannheim, as well as at the Monastery of Our Lady of the Perpetual Rosary in Buffalo, New York, and in various churches. Using patristic thought and art, she recovers *The Key to the Brescia Casket:Typology and the Early Christian Imagination* (Brepols and The University of Notre Dame Press, 2001). Her current research treats Susanna, the heroine of the Book of Daniel.

Notes

1 An example where selection is appropriate is in the direction for the bishop to determine the placement of the tabernacle with reference to, among other concerns, local custom.

2 "Back to the Drawing Board: Rethinking Church Architecture" *Crisis* (February, 2000), 33–38.

3 *Catechism of the Catholic Church* (Città del Vaticano: Libreria Editrice Vaticana, 1994), §774.

4 Robert Hedicke, *Cornelis Floris und die Florisdekoration* (Berlin: Julius Bard, 1913), vol.3:78–86 with plates; Catherine Brown Tkacz, "Susanna as a Type of Christ," *Studies in Iconography* 29 (1999): 101–53, at 129–31 with fig. 11. See also the evidence provided by Jeremy Bangs, *Church Art and Architecture in the Low Countries before the Reformation: The Survivors of 1566* (Ann Arbor: Edwards Brothers, for Sixteenth Century Journal Publications, 1997).

5 Princeton: Princeton University Press, 1997.

6 *Sermo* 300, par. 1.5–6 (PL 38:1379–80), discussed on p. 62 of my essay on "The Seven Maccabees, the Three Hebrews, and a Newly Discovered Sermon of Saint Augustine," *Revue des études augustiniennes* 41.1 (1995) 59–78.

7 "What Happened to Church Architecture?" *Second Spring* (March, 1995), 27–38.

Chapter 7
Cinema: The Power of Visual Imagery
Why There Isn't a Catholic Cinema;
and What Can Happy Catholics Contribute to
the Entertainment Industry?
Barbara R. Nicolosi

Introduction

We are considering in these days the influence of the Catholic imagination in the arts. While there have been isolated instances of film projects that represent a Catholic worldview, the sad reality is that we do not have any filmmakers who have done with cinema what Flannery O'Connor and Graham Greene did in literature, or Fra Angelico in painting, or Bach in sacred music – that is, it is difficult to come up with a single filmmaker who, being what I call a "happy Catholic," has consistently sought to make an appeal for Jesus and the Gospel through mastery of the craft of film. (A "happy Catholic" is one who is distinguished from any of the thousands of people in my experience in the entertainment industry who, under the right circumstances, would identify themselves as Catholic, but who effectively dissent from whichever aspects of the Church's teaching they find inconvenient to themselves or to their friends.)

I run a program in Hollywood to train committed Catholic (and non-Catholic) Christian writers for mainstream Hollywood careers. We have found that the most difficult part of keeping the program going is in simply finding Christian writers who are worth training. Those we identify who have the requisite background in theology and philosophy generally have no interest in evangelizing the popular culture. This is curious to me because clearly, the media of cinema and television are the most potent and influential global pulpits available to disseminate the Catholic imagination.

Too many religious people think that the answer to the "problem of Hollywood" is for a bunch of Catholics to get together, raise some money, and make movies about saints that parents can watch with their four-year olds. Instead, what is needed is for the Church to recognize and respect the power of the cinematic art form, to embrace it, and to send a whole new generation of young artists into the entertainment industry so that, in seeing the good that they do, the culture will give glory to God.

A. This talk will have several parts, including:

B. Attitudes that get in the way of a Catholic cinema.

C. The elements of cinema as a distinct art form.

D. The potential for impact of cinema.

E. What the Church really wants movies to be as art and entertainment.

F. What Catholic filmmakers can bring to the industry.

The Elements of Cinema as an Art Form

Why establish cinema as an art form? Many otherwise intelligent and committed Christians regard cinema and television with a jaundiced eye, or else with a complete lack of respect. My Catholic friends outside the industry are perpetually noting to me with a self-satisfied air, "I never watch television." Or: "I haven't been to the movies for years. It's all garbage."

Many disdain cinema because it has become so tied to pop culture. There was a time when being cultured meant knowing the difference between a Chopin sonata and a Strauss minuet. Being "cultured" today means you know what *The Matrix* is and what makes a current Russell Crowe character's mind so beautiful. There is an elitist attitude in many intellectuals that screen productions are "easy" because they are so ubiquitous. The thinking seems to be that if cinema is that great an art, then the masses should not be able to appreciate it.

Some refuse to confer "fine art status" on screen productions because they are principally generated through a business process. Cinema is almost always a ploy by studios to trade their offerings for dollars, and, consequently, business minds often have as much to say about the artwork in progress as do the artists involved in the project. These realities seem incompatible with the artistic process that for many people is fundamentally an individual act. I have heard several people sniff, "I don't believe in art by committee."

Finally, some people actually think film and television are innately evil. They shudder as at a vision of the apocalypse at the suggestion that ours is becoming a "visually oriented society." "Hollywood" is personified as a united organism of darkness, not only because of the emanations on the screen of the liberal Democratic agenda that is the ideology of choice for many in the entertainment universe, but also because of the presumed dangers of the physical passivity that is predicable of screen viewers.

All of these attitudes get in the way of a serious Catholic incursion into the tremendously powerful arena of popular culture. Our best and brightest shy away from or completely ward off the world of media and entertainment – or else they end up leaving behind their Catholic faith in pursuit of their careers as artists.

To those who say, "TV and movies are all garbage," I say, "you are wrong, and you are missing out on much incredibly beautiful and profound work being done both for the cinema and on television." Films like *The Straight Story, O Brother Where Art Thou?, A Beautiful Mind,* and, of course, *The Lord of the Rings,* are serious and well-crafted works of art that have much to offer those of us trying to live a well-examined human life.

To those who disdain popular culture in general, I remind them that Mozart found his greatest success not in the courts of Europe but in the vaudevillian beer-halls of Austria. Cinema has been such a success as an art form, that it has become the entertainment of choice for the masses. Sometimes, things are popular because they are great, like soap or the wheel.

To those who think human advancement must be tied to the printed word, I recommend a bit more respect for the power and potential goodness of visual imagery. It is only recently that mankind has been generally literate, and, frankly, all of our books haven't made us any more virtuous than men were in the past. From the medieval mystery plays to the stained glass windows in the Gothic cathedrals, visual media were important catechetical tools for the Church in bygone eras.

I have no idea whether movies and television are innately harmful in an anthropological sense. In my view, they are here, and they aren't going away. I know that they can be used to encourage, edify, deepen, and draw people into communion. I experience them as wonderful means, and here I defer to the Church which has repeatedly called for a Catholic presence in the media in many documents starting with Vatican II's *Inter Mirifica*. In the words of John Paul II to filmmakers: "...You are the stewards and administrators of an immense spiritual power that belongs to the patrimony of mankind and is meant to enrich the whole of the human community" (from an address of Pope John Paul to Hollywood filmmakers on September 15, 1987).

The Elements of Cinema as a Distinct Art Form

If the Church is going to make headway into this art form, than we need to know what it is we are talking about when we talk about cinema. What are the limits and possibilities of the art form as a means of expression?

1. Cinema is a Harmony of Harmonies

Cinema is much more than "a visual medium." Saying cinema is a visual medium is like saying Van Gogh was a painter who worked in yellow. He did, of course, along with every other color in the spectrum. If art is selection, and beauty is harmonious selection, then, a beautiful movie is a harmony of harmonies. A work of cinema includes: literature (screenwriting), composition (painting), acting, architecture and sculpture (set design), hair, makeup and costume design, sound design, photography, musical composition, and computer generated effects. It is hard to come up with an art form that isn't a part of cinema.

A. Visual Aspects of Cinema – The visual elements that a filmmaker can arrange in his movie include the actor's performance, set and production design, costume and make-up design, cinematography, lighting, visual effects, and editing. Having these elements on his palette, there are basically three ways a filmmaker can employ them to convey meaning.

1) Visual Imagery – This involves exploiting a universal symbolic meaning already attached to specific objects or actions, as in a young woman kissing a frog, or else in leading the viewers to accept particular objects as symbols of something new, as in the handful of dirt from Tara that motivates Scarlet in *Gone With the Wind.* In the opening sequence of *The Color Purple*, there is an image of a single purple wildflower and then a sequence of images of a field filled with thousands of purple wildflowers. The flowers are fragile, and as wildflowers, would be considered insignificant in the eyes of the world. But through the filmmaker's creative control, we are forced to consider them and see how beautiful and delicate they are. (As Hitchcock said, "Movies are not just about seeing new things. They are about seeing old things in a new way.") The wildflowers are purple, like bruises and also like the marks of royalty. Purple is the color of sacrifice and repentance.

This sequence of images constitutes the filmmaker's poetry in which the flowers represent the women of the movie. We are going to watch the story of one woman, but there are thousands. These women suffer, but it is a suffering that can lead them to a royal dignity.

2) Composition of Images – This level of communication involves the way that a filmmaker chooses to reveal the images of his story. So, an image of a candle in the darkness means hope on the level of imagery. But if we shoot it from far up in the sky, as a compositional choice, we add an irony to the symbolic dimension and turn the symbol on its head. This tiny flame in a huge dark space seems to be pathetic and hopeless.

In the famous last sequence in *Citizen Kane*, the filmmaker chooses to take us through the warehouse of Kane's collected treasures from the omniscient point of view, from somewhere high up there looking down. This perspective makes all of the stuff below look like so much junk, and expressing powerfully, "Vanity of vanities, all is vanity."

3) Juxtaposition of Images – This involves arranging visuals or sequences of visuals in a paradoxical relationship that conveys meaning. So in the Normandy sequence in *Saving Private Ryan*, a dead soldier lies face down on the beach. This is an image of heroism. But all around him are small dead fish. Dead fish stink. They are throw-a-ways. By placing these two images together, the filmmaker makes a statement about the cost of war: many lives become insignificant throw-a-ways on the way to victory.

B. Aural Aspects of Cinema – These include an actor's performance of dialogue, musical score, sound design and editing.

1) Dialogue – Screen dialogue offers a filmmaker two more levels to communicate with the viewers.

Literal meaning of words – The characters tell us facts like, "John is crazy."

Sub-textual meaning of language – The characters reveal to us their own psychology by making observations that seem to contradict the visuals. This is a kind of communication in which a filmmaker speaks *with character* as opposed to speaking *through character*.

2) Ambient sound – All of the noises that surround the characters in a movie offer a filmmaker more means of communicating meaning. In *Saving Private Ryan*, the rat-a-tat of the machine guns at Normandy fades into the rat-a-tat of the typewriters in the War Department as the young clerks issue death notices. The implication is clearly that war has many casualties beyond those who die on the battlefield. Some people die from bullets, some people will die from death notice letters which will wound them like bullets.

C. New Tactile Potential of Cinema – This is the most recent innovation in the cinematic experience. There are theaters now at theme parks that incorporate tactile sensation into the movie experience. In the Muppet movie theater in Disney's new California Adventure park, when the characters walk through the fog, the audience experiences an actual slimy mist. When characters on the screen are attacked by bees, the audience gets tiny pin pricks through the seatbacks. There is also real wind, the heat of a raging fire and bumping under the floor when the characters get into a crash on the screen.

2. Cinema is a Collaborative Medium

Because so many talents and skill sets are involved in its creation, a motion picture is effectively art by committee. In the industry, a cinema or television project is said to "work" when a vision has been well communicated to a large group, and their contributions complement the initial vision making the whole project an effective unity. The vision isn't lost but expanded.

3. Cinema is Tied to Technology

Very often, people outside the industry disdain the use of special effects in cinema as though these get in the way of the story. They only get in the way of the movie acting like a book, but they certainly don't diminish a movie. They are "movie." They are as much part of the palette of the filmmaker as the blank page is for a novel writer.

The fact is we don't even know what to call the screen art form because it keeps changing. The thing that viewers have gone to enjoy in darkened theaters for the last hundred years has gone from being "Moving Pictures" to "Picture Shows" as in the early days of the Nickelodeon, to Silent Films, to Talkies to Movies to Films with Digital Sound and most recently to the 3-D IMAX projects. Each of these periods has had its own masters and classics. Virginia Woolf complained in the early 1930s that: "The problem with cinema is that its technology is perpetually outgrowing its aesthetic accomplishments." It would be as though every five years, ten new colors were discovered which painters could then use on their canvases.

That cinema is tied to technology does not diminish its stature as an art form. It just makes it harder to follow the development of the art form.

4. Cinema is Modern

Cinema is modern in a philosophical sense as well as in a technological sense. As a completely modern medium, cinema has only existed in the period after modern philosophy proclaimed, "God is dead." All the confusions of this past century have been the subject of the art form. There isn't a Renaissance cinema that would balance out the artistic confusion of the last hundred years, the way Michaelangelo balances out Andy Warhol and thus keeps painting as a fine art in the minds of contemporary Christians.

5. Cinema is the Product of a Business

As an art form, cinema is like architecture in that the palette and canvas of the artist represents a huge investment. A recent article in the industry trades noted that due to the advances in digital editing technology the average cost of making a movie has fallen "way down" in recent years to just around $26 million dollars. Because they are so expensive to produce, there is always a commercial aspect involved in shaping a movie. This is often a positive thing as it functions as a means to maintain quality control. If you have to sell something, than it has to have something of the beautiful or at least well-crafted to attract buyers.

6. Cinema Is an Art Form that Is Consumed by Many as Entertainment.

There is a perpetual tension between Hollywood cinema that is based in stories, and the cinema propounded by artists from the rest of the planet who regard storytelling as a bastardization of cinema –

forcing upon it the substance of other art forms like literature and theater. There is no either/or. Cinema is an art. Cinema is entertainment.

This tension is the source of many of the Church's troubles with "Hollywood." As members of the human family, we understand that there are legitimate and illegitimate ways in which to entertain people. But every time we culturally concerned people raise the subject of how to regulate entertainment, we bang into the fact that cinema is an art form, and as such must be respected as a free form of expression. Trying to censor or regulate filmmakers is arrogant and dangerous. Because He values our freedom as the essential element to his whole human project thing, God lets us sin. The Church needs to weather the same risk with artists.

Impact of the Art Form

As an aggregate of many art forms, a movie has access to all of the power that each individual art form brings with it to move the human heart. Flannery O'Connor indicates that the fundamental power in literature resides in setting up a paradox that traps a reader into a journey of discovery.

From my own experience in trying to make stories "work," I have discovered that what is needed is an action that is totally unexpected, yet totally believable ... It would have to one that is both in character and beyond character; it would have to suggest both the world and eternity ... It would be a gesture which somehow made contact with mystery. *(Flannery O'Connor, Mystery and Manners)*

Cinema has the possibility to develop more complex paradoxes than any other art form by setting the different levels of meaning present in a movie up against one another either complementarily or through contrast. A complex visual image can be achieved by combining symbolism, composition, and juxtaposition. This can then be contrasted with contrasting dialogue and ambient sounds. The whole thing can be accompanied with a musical score that adds a further layer of meaning until what is achieved is an immensely complex, and layered project that speaks to a viewer on a constantly shifting number of levels.

What a Catholic Cinema Would Look Like

1. Entertainment Versus Amusement

I recently spoke to a television sit-com writer, suggesting that he might try to write with a concern for the impact of his comedy on his audience. He replied to me, "In twelve years of writing for television, it never occurred to me to aspire to anything except keeping the viewer from turning the channel." His goal has only ever been to amuse people in the sense of filling up their time, distracting them, but with little or no view to giving them anything lasting or helpful in living out their lives.

A Catholic sensibility would bring to Hollywood the certainty that entertainment time is not wasted time. The word entertainment comes from a French word meaning "the work between the work." As Catholic philosopher Josef Pieper noted, "Leisure is the basis of culture," because in it, we find meaning and depth that can then animate the workaday world. An essential element of a healthy human life is entertainment that is recreative; times of awe and wonder, times of self-discovery and giving birth.

2. Cinema as Pre-Evangelization Not Catechesis

We will always need churches. The goal of our efforts in media is not to replace what happens at church, in terms of preaching. Cinema should incite people to begin a search that leads them to the Church. Cinema can deepen believers so that what they experience at Church is more profound. Cinema can model the consequences of a Gospel worldview versus a completely materialist worldview.

The elements of a Catholic worldview are beyond our scope here, but would include a sense of sacramentality, an "at homeness" with mystery, a conviction of connectedness and responsibility for others, a lasting hope.

Catholic filmmakers have an innate ability to construct effective visual images because of the liturgy that has come to us through the Church. We have been raised in a climate of metaphor and symbolism that we have experienced as powerful and so we trust it to convey meaning. My experience with Evangelical Christianity is that they are suspicious of images as not being sufficient to "get the job done."

3. The Filmmaker as "The Aroma of Christ" in the Industry

The principal reason for the moral confusion that ends up on the screen is the paucity of happy, well-catechized believers in the entertainment industry. We do not have enough witnesses to Christ living and loving and working alongside the witnesses to Mammon or secular humanism that have overrun the creative community. We do not need a "Catholic Cinema" so much as we need Catholics in cinema.

We do not need the Church to set up production companies and make movies. We need the Church to approach Hollywood as a missionary territory; to preach and teach and minister – so that the people in the arts and entertainment can make movies for us.

Barbara R. Nicolosi is the founding director of *Act One: Writing for Hollywood*, a program sponsored by Inter-Mission and the Catholic Communication Campaign to train screenwriters from the Christian community for mainstream entertainment industry careers. Formerly the director of project development for Paulist Productions (*Romero, Entertaining Angels: The Dorothy Day Story*), she has consulted on numerous feature length and television projects. Her screenplay *Select Society,* about Emily Dickinson, is in development with a Los Angeles production company.

Ms. Nicolosi is on the board of Catholics in Media Associates and on the Executive Committee for the City of the Angels Film Festival. She has been a judge for the Humanitas Prize for screen writing and is on the film juries for the Gabriel Awards and the Angelus Awards. She writes a monthly column on media in the national magazine *Liguorian*, and frequently lectures on culture and the arts. She has an M.A. in television and film from Northwestern University in Evanston, Illinois.

Chapter 8
The Music of the Spheres;
Or, The Metaphysics of Music
Robert R. Reilly

I.

Despite the popular Romantic conception of creative artists as madmen, composers are not idiots savants, distilling their musical inspiration from the ether. Rather, in their creative work, they respond and give voice to certain metaphysical visions. Most composers speak explicitly in philosophical terms about the nature of the reality that they try to reflect. When the forms of musical expression change radically, it is always because the underlying metaphysical grasp of reality has changed as well. Music is, in a way, the sound of metaphysics, or metaphysics in sound.

Music in the Western world was shaped by a shared conception of reality so profound that it endured for some twenty-five hundred years. As a result, the means of music remained essentially the same – at least to the extent that what was called music could always have been recognized as such by its forbears (as much as they might have disapproved of its specific style). By the early 20th century, this was no longer true. Music was re-conceptualized so completely that it could no longer be experienced as music, i.e., with melody, harmony, and rhythm. This catastrophic rupture, expressed especially in the works of Arnold Schoenberg and John Cage, is often celebrated as just another change in the techniques of music, a further point along the parade of progress in the arts. It was, however, a reflection of a deeper metaphysical divide that severed the composer from any meaningful contact with external reality. As a result, musical art was reduced to the arbitrary manipulation of fragments of sound.

This essay will give a sketch of the philosophical presuppositions that undergirded the Western conception of music for most of its existence, and then will examine the character of the change music underwent in the 20th century. It will end with a reflection on the recovery of music in our own time, and the reasons for it, as exemplified in the works of two contemporary composers, the Danish Vagn Holmboe and the American John Adams.

According to tradition, the harmonic structure of music was discovered by Pythagoras around the 5th century B.C. Pythagoras experimented with a stretched piece of cord. When plucked, the cord sounded a certain note. When halved in length and plucked again, the cord sounded a higher note completely consonant with the first. In fact, it was the same note at a higher pitch. Pythagoras had discovered the ratio, 2:1, of the octave. Further experiments, plucking the string two-thirds of its original length produced a perfect fifth in the ratio of 3:2. When a three-quarters length of cord was plucked, a perfect fourth was sounded in the ratio of 4:3, and so forth. These sounds were all consonant and extremely pleasing to the ear. The significance that Pythagoras attributed to this discovery cannot be overestimated. Pythagoras thought that number was the key to the universe. When he found that harmonic music is expressed in exact numerical ratios of whole numbers, he concluded that music was the ordering principle of the world. The fact that music was denominated in exact numerical ratios demonstrated to him the intelligibility of reality and the existence of a reasoning intelligence behind it.

Pythagoras wondered about the relationship of these ratios to the larger world. (The Greek word for ratio is *logos*, which also means "word," or "reason.") He construed that the harmonious sounds that men could make, either with their instruments or their singing, were an approximation of a larger harmony that existed in the universe, also expressed by numbers, that was exemplified in "the music of the spheres." As Aristotle explained in the *Metaphysics*, the Pythagoreans "supposed the elements of numbers to be the elements of all things, and the whole heaven to be a musical scale and a number." This was meant literally. The heavenly spheres and their rotations through the sky produced tones at various levels, and in concert, these tones made a harmonious sound that man's music, at its best, could approximate. Music was number made audible. Music was man's participation in the harmony of the universe.

This discovery was fraught with ethical significance. By participating in heavenly harmony, music could induce spiritual harmony in the soul. Following Pythagoras, Plato taught that "rhythm and harmony find their way into the inward places of the soul, on which they mightily fasten, imparting grace, and making the soul of him who is rightly educated graceful." In the *Republic*, Plato showed the political import of music's power by invoking Damon of Athens as his musical authority. Damon said that he would rather control the modes of music in a city than its laws, because the modes of music have a more decisive effect on the formation of the character of citizens. The ancient Greeks were also wary of music's power because they understood that, just as there was harmony, so there was disharmony. Musical discord could distort the spirit, just as musical concord could properly dispose it.

This idea of "the music of the spheres" runs through the history of Western civilization with an extraordinary consistency, even up to the 20th century. At first, it was meant literally, later, poetically. Either way, music was seen as more a discovery than a creation, because it relied on pre-existing principles of order in nature for its operation. It would be instructive to look briefly at the reiteration of this teaching in the writings of several major thinkers to appreciate its enduring significance and also the radical nature of the challenge to it in the 20th century.

In the 1st century B.C., Cicero spelled out Plato's teaching in the last chapter of his *De Republica*. In "Scipio's Dream," Cicero has Scipio Africanus asking the question, "What is that great and pleasing sound?" The answer comes, "That is the concord of tones separated by unequal but nevertheless carefully proportional intervals, caused by the rapid motion of the spheres themselves ... Skilled men imitating this harmony on stringed instruments and in singing have gained for themselves a return to this region, as have those who have cultivated their exceptional abilities to search for divine truths." Cicero claims that music can return man to a paradise lost. It is a form of communion with divine truth.

In the late 2nd century A.D., Clement of Alexandria baptized the classical Greek and Roman understanding of music in his *Exhortation to the Greeks*. The transcendent God of Christianity gave new and somewhat different meanings to the "music of the spheres." Using Old Testament imagery from the Psalms, Clement said that there is a "New Song," far superior to the Orphic myths of the pagans. The "New Song" is Christ, *Logos* Himself: "it is this ["New Song"] that composed the entire creation into melodious order, and tuned into concert the discord of the elements, that the whole universe may be in harmony with it." It is Christ who "arranged in harmonious order this great world, yes, and the little world of man, body and soul together; and on this many-voiced instrument he makes music to God and sings to [the accompaniment of] the human instrument." By appropriating the classical view, Clement was able to show that music participated in the divine by praising God and partaking in the harmonious order of which He was the composer. But music's goal was now higher, because Christ is higher. Cicero had spoken of the divine region to which music is supposed to transport man. That region was literally within the heavens. With Christianity, the divine region becomes both transcendent and personal because *Logos* is Christ. The new purpose of music is to make the transcendent perceptible in the "New Song."

The early 6th century A.D. had two especially distinguished Roman proponents of the classical view of music, both of whom served at various times in high offices to the Ostrogoth king, Theodoric. Cassiodorus was secretary to Theodoric. He wrote a massive work called *Institutiones*, which echoes Plato's teaching on the ethical content of music, as well as Pythagoras's on the power of number. Cassiodorus taught that "music indeed is the knowledge of apt modulation. If we live virtuously, we are constantly proved to be under its discipline, but when we sin, we are without music. The heavens and the earth and indeed all things in them which are directed by a higher power share in the discipline of music, for Pythagoras attests that this universe was founded by and can be governed by music."

Boethius served as consul to Theodoric in 510 A.D. He wrote *The Principles of Music*, a book that had enormous influence through the Middle Ages and beyond. Boethius said that "music is related not only to speculation, but to morality as well, for nothing is more consistent with human nature than to be soothed by sweet modes and disturbed by their opposites. Thus, we can begin to understand the apt doctrine of Plato, which holds that the whole of the universe is united by a musical concord. For when we compare that which is coherently and harmoniously joined together within our own being with that which is coherently and harmoniously joined together in sound – that is, that which gives us pleasure – so we come to recognize that we ourselves are united according to the same principle of similarity." It is not necessary to cite further examples after Boethius because *The Principles of Music* was so influential that it held sway as the standard music theory text at Oxford until 1856.

The hieratic role of music even survived into the 20th century with composers like Jean Sibelius. Sibelius harkened back to Clement of Alexandria when he wrote that "the essence of man's being is his striving after God. It [the composition of music] is brought to life by means of the *logos*, the divine in art. That is the only thing that has significance." But this vision was lost for most of the 20th century because the belief on which it was based was lost.

Philosophical propositions have a very direct and profound impact upon composers and what they do. John Adams, one of the most popular American composers today, said that he had "learned in college that tonality died somewhere around the time that Nietzsche's God died, and I believed it." The connection is quite compelling. At the same time God disappears, so does the intelligible order in creation. If there is no God, Nature no longer serves as a reflection of its Creator. If you lose the *Logos* of Clement, you also lose the ratio (*logos*) of Pythagoras. Nature is stripped of its normative power. This is just as much a problem for music as it is for philosophy.

The systematic fragmentation of music was the logical working out of the premise that music is not governed by mathematical relationships and laws that inhere in the structure of a hierarchical and ordered universe, but is wholly constructed by man and therefore essentially without limits or definition. Tonality, as the pre-existing principle of order in the world of sound, goes the same way as the objective moral order. So how does one organize the mess that is left once God departs? If there is no pre-existing intelligible order to go out to and apprehend, and to search through for what lies beyond it – which is the Creator – what then is music supposed to express? If external order does not exist, then music turns inward. It collapses in on itself and becomes an obsession with techniques. Any ordering of things, musical or otherwise, becomes simply the whim of man's will.

II.

Without a "music of the spheres" to approximate, modern music, like the other arts, began to unravel. Music's self-destruction became logically imperative once it undermined its own foundation. In the 1920s, Arnold Schoenberg unleashed the centrifugal forces of disintegration in music through his denial of tonality. Schoenberg contended that tonality does not exist in nature as the very property of sound itself, as Pythagoras claimed, but was simply an arbitrary construct of man, a convention. This assertion was not the result of a new scientific discovery about the acoustical nature of sound, but of a desire to demote the metaphysical status of nature. Schoenberg was irritated that "tonality does not serve, [but] must be served." Rather than conform himself to reality, he preferred to command reality to conform itself to him. As he said, "I can provide rules for almost anything." Like Pythagoras, Schoenberg believed that number was the key to the universe. Unlike Pythagoras, though, he believed his manipulation of number could alter that reality in a profound way. Schoenberg's gnostic impulse is confirmed by his extraordinary obsession with numerology, which would not allow him to finish a composition until its opus number corresponded with the correct number of the calendar date.

Schoenberg proposed to erase the distinction between tonality and atonality by immersing man in atonal music until, through habituation, it became the new convention. Then discords would be heard as concords. As he wrote: "The emancipation of dissonance is at present accomplished and twelve-tone music in the near future will no longer be rejected because of 'discords.'" Anyone who claims that, through his system, the listener shall hear dissonance as consonance is engaged in reconstituting reality.

Of his achievement, Schoenberg said, "I am conscious of having removed all traces of a past aesthetic." In fact, he declared himself "cured of the delusion that the artist's aim is to create beauty." This statement is literally terrifying in its implications when one considers what is at stake in beauty. Simone Weil wrote that "we love the beauty of the world because we sense behind it the presence of something akin to that wisdom we should like to possess to slake our thirst for good." All beauty is reflected beauty. Smudge out the reflection and not only is the mirror useless, but the path to the source of beauty is barred. Ugliness, the aesthetic analogue to evil, becomes the new norm. Schoenberg's remark represents a total rupture with Western musical tradition.

The loss of tonality was also devastating at the practical level of composition because tonality is the key structure of music.

Schoenberg took the twelve equal semi-tones from the chromatic scale and declared that music must be written in such a way that each of these twelve semi-tones has to be used before repeating any one of them. If one of these semi-tones was repeated before all eleven others were sounded, it might create an anchor for the ear which could recognize what is going on in the music harmonically. The twelve-tone system guarantees the listener's disorientation.

Tonality is what allows music to express movement, away from or towards a state of tension or relaxation, a sense of motion through a series of crises and conflicts, which can then come to resolution. Without it, music loses harmony and melody. Its structural force collapses. Gutting music of tonality is like removing grapes from wine. You can go through all the motions of making wine without grapes but there will be no wine at the end of the process. Similarly, if you deliberately and systematically remove all audible overtone relationships from music, you can go though the process of composition, but the end product will not be comprehensible as music. This is not a change in technique; it is the replacement of art by ideology.

Schoenberg's disciples applauded the emancipation of dissonance, but soon preferred to follow the centrifugal forces that Schoenberg had unleashed beyond their master's rules. Pierre Boulez thought that it was not enough to systematize dissonance in twelve-tone rows. If you have a system, why not systematize everything? He applied the same principle of the tone-row to pitch, duration, tone production, intensity and timber, every element of music. In 1952, Boulez announced that "every musician who has not felt – we do not say understood but felt – the necessity of the serial language is USELESS." Boulez also proclaimed, "Once the past has been got out of the way, one need think only of oneself." Here is the narcissistic antithesis of the classical view of music, the whole point of which was to catch a person up into something larger than himself.

The dissection of the language of music continued as, successively, each isolated element was elevated into its own autonomous whole. Schoenberg's disciples agreed that tonality is simply a convention, but saw that, so too, is twelve-tone music. If you are going to emancipate dissonance, why organize it? Why even have twelve-tone themes? Why bother with pitch at all? Edgar Varese rejected the twelve-tone system as arbitrary and restrictive. He searched for the "bomb that would explode the musical world and allow all sounds to come rushing into it through the resulting breach." When he exploded it in his piece, *Ameriques*, Olin Downes, a famous New York music critic, called it "a catastrophe in a boiler factory." Still Varese did not carry the inner logic of the "emancipation of dissonance" through to its logical conclusion. His noise was still formulated; it was organized. There were indications in the score as to exactly when the boiler should explode.

What was needed, according to John Cage (1912–1992), was to have absolutely no organization. Typical of Cage were compositions whose notes were based on the irregularities in the composition paper he used, notes selected by tossing dice, or from the use of charts derived from the Chinese *I Ching*. Those were his more conventional works. Other "compositions" included the simultaneous twirling of the knobs of twelve radios, the sounds from records playing on unsynchronized variable speed turntables, or the sounds produced by tape recordings of music that had been sliced up and randomly reassembled. Not surprisingly, Cage was one of the progenitors of the "happenings" that were fashionable in the 1970s. He presented concerts of kitchen sounds and sounds of the human body amplified through loudspeakers. Perhaps Cage's most notorious work was his *4'33"* during which the performer silently sits with his instrument for that exact period of time, then rises and leaves the stage. The "music" is whatever extraneous noises the audience hears in the silence the performer has created. In his book, *Silence*, Cage announced: "Here we are. Let us say *Yes* to our presence together in Chaos."

What was the purpose of all this? Precisely to make the point that there is no purpose, or to express what Cage called a "purposeful purposelessness," the aim of which was to emancipate people from the tyranny of meaning. The extent of his success can be judged by the verdict rendered in the prestigious *New Grove Dictionary of Music*, which says Cage "has had a greater impact on world music than any other American composer of the 20th century." Cage's view of reality has a very clear provenance. Cage himself acknowledged three principal gurus: French composer Eric Satie, Henry David Thoreau, and Buckminister Fuller – three relative lightweights, who could not among them account for Cage's radical thinking. The prevalent influence on Cage seems to have been Jean Jacques Rousseau, though he goes unmentioned in Cage's many obiter dicta.

Cage's similarities with Rousseau are too uncanny to have been accidental.

With his noise, Cage worked out musically the full implications of Rousseau's non-teleological view of nature in Rousseau's Second Discourse. Cage did for music what Rousseau did for philosophy. Perhaps the most profoundly anti-Aristotelian philosopher of the 18th century, Rousseau turned Aristotle's notion of nature on its head. Aristotle said nature defined not only what man is, but what he should be. Rousseau countered that nature is not an end – a telos – but a beginning: man's end is his beginning. There is nothing he "ought" to become, no moral imperative. There is no purpose in man or nature; existence is therefore bereft of any rational principle. Rousseau asserted that man by nature was not a social, political animal endowed with reason. What man has become is the result, not of nature, but of accident. The society resulting from that accident has corrupted man.

According to Rousseau, man was originally isolated in the state of nature, where the pure "sentiment of his own existence" was such that "one suffices to oneself, like God." Yet, this self-satisfied god was asocial and pre-rational. Only by accident did man come into association with others. Somehow, this accident ignited his reason. Through his association with others, man lost his self-sufficient "sentiment of his own existence." He became alienated. He began to live in the esteem of others instead of in his own self-esteem.

Rousseau knew that the pre-rational, asocial state of nature was lost forever, but thought that an all-powerful state could ameliorate the situation of alienated man. The state could restore a simulacrum of that original well-being by removing all man's subsidiary social relationships. By destroying man's familial, social and political ties, the state could make each individual totally dependent on the state, and independent of each other. The state is the vehicle for bringing people together so they can be apart: a sort of radical individualism under state sponsorship.

It is necessary to pay this much attention to Rousseau because Cage shares his denigration of reason, the same notion of alienation, and a similar solution to it. In both men, the primacy of the accidental eliminates nature as a normative guide and becomes the foundation for man's total freedom. Like Rousseau's man in the state of nature, Cage said, "I strive toward the non-mental." The quest is to "provide a music free from one's memory and imagination." If man is the product of accident, his music should likewise be accidental. Life itself is very fine "once one gets one's mind and one's desires out of the way and lets it act of its own accord."

But what is its own accord? Of music, Cage said, "The requiring that many parts be played in a particular togetherness is not an accurate representation of how things are" in nature, because in nature there is no order. In other words, life's accord is that there is no accord. As a result, Cage desired "a society where you can do anything at all." He warned that one has "to be as careful as possible not to form any ideas about what each person should or should not do." He was "committed to letting everything happen, to making everything that happens acceptable."

At the Stony Point experimental arts community where he spent his summers, Cage observed that each summer's sabbatical produced numerous divorces. So, he concluded, "all the couples who come to the community and stay there end up separating. In reality, our community is a community for separation." Rousseau could not have stated his ideal better. Nor could Cage have made the same point in his art more clearly. For instance, in his long collaboration with choreographer Merce Cunningham, Cage wrote ballet scores completely unconnected to and independent of Cunningham's choreography. The orchestra and dancers rehearsed separately and appeared together for the first time at the premiere performance. The dancers' movements have nothing to do with the music. The audience is left to make of these random juxtapositions what it will. There is no shared experience – except of disconnectedness. The dancers, musicians, and audience have all come together in order to be apart.

According to Cage, the realization of the disconnectedness of things creates opportunities for wholeness. "I said that since the sounds were sounds this gave people hearing them the chance to be people, centered within themselves where they actually are, not off artificially in the distance as they are accustomed to be, trying to figure out what is being said by some artist by means of sounds." Here, in his own way, Cage captures Rousseau's notion of alienation. People are alienated from themselves because they are living in the esteem of others. Cage's noise can help them let go of false notions of order, to "let sounds be themselves, rather than vehicles for manmade theories," and to return within themselves to the sentiment of their own existence. Cage said, "Our intention is to affirm this life, not bring order out of chaos or to suggest improvements in creation, but simply to wake up to the very life we're living, which is so excellent...."

That sounds appealing, even humble, and helps to explain Cage's appeal. In fact, Cage repeatedly insisted on the integrity of external reality, which exists without our permission. It is a good point to make and, as far as it goes, protects us from solipsists of every stripe. Man violates this integrity by projecting meanings upon external reality that are not there. This, of course, is the distortion of reality at the heart of every modern ideology. For Cage, however, it is the inference of meaning itself that is the distorting imposition. This is the real problem with letting "sounds be themselves," and letting other things be as they are, because it begs the question, "what are they?" Because of Cage's grounding in Rousseau, we cannot answer this question. What is the significance of reality's integrity if it is not intelligible, if there is not a rational principle animating it? If creation does not speak to us in some way, if things are not intelligible, are we? Where does "leaving things as they are" leave us?

From the traditional Western perspective, it leaves us completely adrift. The Greco-Judeo-Christian conviction is that nature bespeaks an intelligibility that derives from a transcendent source. Speaking from the heart of that tradition, St. Paul in Romans said, "ever since the creation of the world, the invisible existence of God and his everlasting power have been clearly seen by the mind's understanding of created things." By denigrating reason and denying creation's intelligibility, Cage severed this link to the Creator. Cage's espousal of accidental noise is the logically apt result of this. Noise is incapable of pointing beyond itself. Noise is the black hole of the sound world. It sucks everything into itself. If reality is unintelligible, then noise is its perfect reflection because it too is unintelligible.

III.

Having endured the worst, the 20th century has also witnessed an extraordinary recovery from the damage inflicted by Schoenberg in his totalitarian systematization of sound and by Cage in his mindless immersion in noise. Some composers, like Vagn Holmboe (1909–1996) in Denmark, resisted from the start. Others, like John Adams (b.1947) in America, rebelled and returned to tonal music. It is worth examining, even briefly, the terms of this recovery in the works of these two composers because their language reconnects us to the worlds of Pythagoras and Clement of Alexandria. Their works are symptomatic of the broader recovery of reality in the music of our time.

In Vagn Holmboe's music, most particularly in his thirteen symphonies, one can once again detect the "music of the spheres" in their rotation. Holmboe's impulse was to move outward and upward. His music reveals the constellations in their swirling orbits, cosmic forces, a universe of tremendous complexity, but also of coherence. Holmboe's music is rooted and real. It reflects nature, but not in a pastoral way; this is not a musical evocation of bird song or sunsets. Neither is it nature as the 19th century understood nature – principally as a landscape upon which to project one's own emotions. To say his work is visionary would be an understatement.

Holmboe's approach to composition was quite Aristotelian: the thematic material defines its own development. What a thing is (its essence), is fully revealed through its completion (its existence), through the thorough exploration of the potential of its basic materials. The overall effect is cumulative and the impact powerful. Holmboe found his unique voice through a technique he called metamorphosis. Holmboe wrote, "metamorphosis is based on a process of development that transforms one matter into another, without it losing its identity." Most importantly, metamorphosis "has a goal; it brings order to the process and enables it to create a pattern of the same perfection and balance as, for example, a classical sonata." Holmboe's metamorphosis is something like the Beethovenian method of arguing short motives; a few hammered chords can generate the thematic material for the whole work.

Holmboe's technique also has a larger significance. Danish composer Karl Aage Rasmussen observed that Holmboe's metamorphosis has striking similarities with the constructive principles employed by Arnold Schoenberg in his 12–tone music. However, says Rasmussen, "Schoenberg found his arguments in history while Holmboe's come from nature." This difference is decisive since the distinction is metaphysical. History is the authority for those, like Rousseau, who believe that man's nature is the product of accident and, therefore, malleable. Nature is the authority for those who believe man's essence is permanently ordered to a transcendent good. The argument from history leads to creation *ex nihilo*, not so much in imitation of God as a replacement for Him – as was evident in the ideologies of Marxism and Nazism that plagued the 20th century. The argument from nature leads to creation in cooperation with the Creator.

Rasmussen spelled out exactly the theological implications of Holmboe's approach: "The voice of nature is heard ...both as an inner impulse and as spokesman for a higher order. Certainty of this order is the stimulus of music, and to recreate it and mirror it is the highest goal. For this, faith is required, faith in meaning and context or, in Holmboe's own words, "cosmos does not develop from chaos without a prior vision of cosmos." Holmboe's words could come straight from one of Aquinas's proofs for the existence of God. For Holmboe to make such a remark reveals both his metaphysical grounding and his breathtaking artistic reach. This man was not simply reaching for the stars, but for the constellations in which they move, and beyond. Holmboe strove to show us the cosmos, to play for us the music of the spheres.

Holmboe's music is quite accessible but requires a great deal of concentration because it is highly contrapuntal. Its rich counterpoint reflects creation's complexity. The simultaneity of unrelated strands of music in so much modern music (as in John Cage's works) is no great accomplishment; relating them is. As Holmboe said, music has the power to enrich man "only when the music itself is a cosmos of coordinated powers, when it speaks to both feeling and thought, when chaos does exist, but [is] always overcome."

In other words, chaos is not the problem; chaos is easy. Cosmos is the problem. Showing the coherence in its complexity, to say nothing of the reason for its existence, is the greatest intellectual and artistic challenge because it shares in the divine "prior vision of cosmos" that makes the cosmos possible. As Holmboe wrote, "In its purest form, [music] can be regarded as the expression of a perfect unity and conjures up a feeling of cosmic cohesion." Arising from such complexity, this feeling of cohesion can be, he said, a "spiritual shock" for modern man.

Just as Holmboe, whose magnificent works are finally coming into currency, represents an unbroken line to the great Western musical tradition, so John Adams is an exemplar of those indoctrinated in Schoenberg's ideology who found their way out of it. Adams ultimately rejected his college lessons on Nietzsche's "death of God" and the loss of tonality. Like Pythagoras, he "found that tonality was not just a stylistic phenomenon that came and went, but that it is really a natural acoustic phenomenon." In total repudiation of Schoenberg, Adams went on to write a stunning symphony, entitled *Harmonielehre (Theory of Harmony)* that powerfully reconnects with the Western musical tradition. In this work, he wrote, "there is a sense of using key as a structural and psychological tool in building my work." More importantly, Adams explained, "the other shade of meaning in the title has to do with harmony in the larger sense, in the sense of spiritual and psychological harmony."

Adam's description of his symphony is explicitly in terms of spiritual health and sickness. He explains that "the entire [second] movement is a musical scenario about impotence and spiritual sickness ... it has to do with an existence without grace. And then in the third movement, grace appears for no reason at all ... that's the way grace is, the unmerited bestowal of blessing on man. The whole piece is a kind of allegory about that quest for grace."

It is clear from Adams that the recovery of tonality and key structure is as closely related to spiritual recovery as its loss was related to spiritual loss. The destruction of tonality was thought to be historically necessary and therefore "determined." It is no mistake that the recovery of tonality and its expressive powers should be accompanied by the notion of grace. The very possibility of grace, of the unmerited intervention of God's love, destroys the ideology of historical determinism, whether it be expressed in music or in any other way. The possibility of grace fatally ruptures the self-enclosed world of "historically determined forces" and opens it up to the transcendent. That opening restores the freedom and full range of man's creativity.

Cicero spoke of music as enabling man to *return* to the divine region, implying a place once lost to man. What is it, in and about music, that gives one an experience so outside of oneself that one can see reality anew, as if newborn in a strange but wonderful world? British composer John Tavener proposes an answer to this mystery in his artistic credo: "My goal is to recover one simple memory from which all art derives. The constant memory of the paradise from which we have fallen leads to the paradise which was promised to the repentant thief. The gentleness of our sleepy recollections promises something else. That which was once perceived as in a glass darkly, we shall see face to face." We shall not only *see*; we shall *hear*, as well, the New Song.

Just days after delivering the above lecture at the 2001 Omaha conference of the Fellowship of Catholic Scholars, Robert R. Reilly was named by President George W. Bush to be the new Director of the Voice of America. Prior to that he was the producer and program host of "On the Line," a weekly radio and television foreign-policy talk show. Previously, he was producer and program host of "Vineline."

Mr. Reilly has also served as president of the Intercollegiate Studies Institute in Bryn Mawr, Pennsylvania. In the Reagan Administration, among other positions he served as Senior Advisor for Public Diplomacy at the U.S. Embassy in Bern, Switzerland, and as a Special Assistant to the President in Washington, D.C. He has a B.A. in English from Georgetown University and an M.A. in Political Science from the Claremont Graduate School.

For a number of years he has been a contributing editor and music critic for *Crisis* magazine, and continues to write his monthly music column while serving as Director of the Voice of America. He is founder and chairman of the Committee for Western Civilization, and a member of the Republican National Committee's Catholic Task Force. His publications include: *We Hold These Truths, The Truths They Hold, The Fall of the Wall, The New Federalist Papers,* and *The Spirit of Music.* He and his wife are the parents of three children.

Chapter 9
Response to Robert R. Reilly's
"The Music of the Spheres"
Rev. Basil Cole, O.P.

I wish to thank Mr. Reilly for bringing to our attention some aspects of the problems facing music as an art in today's modern world. My remarks will be to further complement, explain, or distinguish some of his basic premises in his fine paper.

I think Mary Louise Serafine has expressed quite well the mystery of how music becomes beautiful.

> It is not clear what we are doing when we engage in music-making. It is not at all clear why music affects us. In creating and listening to music, we experience organization, coherence, and deviation, but it is not immediately obvious how such effects are caused, or where in the music they lie. Music is all the more difficult to pin down on this matter because it is a passing, temporal thing that will not hold still while we look at it. We cannot stop it at some point and say, "there, *that* is the pattern ... the repetition ... the form," for whatever we point to evaporates and is lost. Music unfolds in temporal experience; it is always continuous and in flux. Still, we have the definite impression that music involves a characteristic experience, principally one in which the flow of temporal events is organized in some way.[1]

In some ways, the musician's works are similar to metaphysics because as Jacques Maritain puts it: " ... So music perhaps more than any other art gives us an enjoyment of being, but does not give us knowledge of being, and it would be absurd to make music a substitute for metaphysics...."[2] If the musician is someone who forges melody, harmony, pauses, counter point, degrees of softness and loudness, tonal color of various instruments, and rhythm in such a way as to bring about unity, harmony, splendor, integrity, the metaphysics, if you will, of beauty according to Thomas, he is very close to the metaphysical mind. However, one should not too easily believe the musician when he tries to articulate his philosophy of music, since he does not always have a talent for philosophizing.

St. Thomas Aquinas, like his predecessors on these questions, speaks of actually composing melodies as a path which introduces a young mind to the secrets of philosophy since it is one of the liberal arts (*In Boeth. de Trin.*, 5,1, ad 3). Yet it is interesting that Aristotle did not recommend composing, but preferred training youth to play the music already given them by tradition.

We also need to keep in mind that musicians and poets are almost the same persons in the early Greek culture. By the time of Plato, they begin to become distinct.[3] Poetry and music go together so closely that one includes the other, making it difficult for any philosopher to uncover exactly what is the meaning of music as such. Pure music or wordless music was not thought to be an important subject matter for reflection by the philosophers until the eighteenth century.

As Mr. Reilly referred us to Pythagoras, this philosopher is really the father of Greek music science (Sixth Century B.C.). However, his writings no longer exist though his ideas are found and commented on by both Plato and Aristotle, among many other later philosophers, including Iamblicus and Boethius. On the question of the harmony of the spheres, he succeeds in convincing Plato, Cicero, Macrobius, and Boethius, but not Aristotle who ridicules it (see *De caelo* II, 9, 290b 12). (St. Thomas follows Aristotle on this question.) For Pythagoras, music must be an imitation of the unheard harmony of the spheres (similar to a Chinese notion). Moreover, he strongly influences everyone until the late 18th century by teaching that certain modes of music influence behavior. Plato constructs his notion of the world-soul by using a metaphor of music as harmonizing ingredients of the consonances in tuning stringed instruments, which was taught by Pythagoras (*Tim.* 35b–36). In fact, in the creation account of the *Timaeus*, he makes extensive use of Pythagorean imagery of music.

But when speculating about Greek music, musicologists remind us that a theory of music is "dead" until it is illustrated by real melodies.[4] Unfortunately, we do not know exactly what the music of the Greeks sounded like. What few theories exist are rejected by an overwhelming number of musicologists. Moreover, although musicologists know more about the first twelve centuries since Christianity than the previous centuries of Greece or China, it must be kept in mind that no developed system of notation of melodies and rests within musical compositions existed until the tenth century when Guido of Arezzo introduced its beginnings.[5] Harmony as we know it came even later.

Now after the fall of Athens, we find the ability of poets to write music and the ability of musicians to write poetry declined, which shows how deeply music and poetry were entwined.[6] Likewise, Winnington-Ingram demonstrates clearly that *harmoniae and tonoie* means something quite different than mere "harmony and tone." The Greeks did not use scales, and *tonoi* were tunings of the *kithara* to be played.[7] Therefore, concerning the doctrine of ethos and the modes having definite moral and psychological effects, the following from Hollander explains very profoundly how to understand what they are talking about: "The whole notion of musical effect [was] intimately involved with the sense of the text, and ultimately, the meaning of the words."[8] And Winn's comment also explains the meaning of the modes when he says: "Thus Plato's famous exclusion of all *harmoniai* except the Dorian and Phrygian from his *Republic* is less a claim that these melodic idioms were noble or manly in themselves than an acknowledgement that the Dorian and Phrygian *harmoniae* had traditionally been used in association with serious and patriotic texts; the *harmoniai* he excludes, such as the Mixolydian, had been associated with shrill dirges."[9]

Pythagoras was the first among the Greeks of whom we know to develop the idea of music as ethical and therapeutic, capable of strengthening or restoring harmony to the soul.[10] He probably formulated his ideas to recommend a definite mode of life based on the premise that man's soul is a harmony called virtue. Order, proportion and measure are the essence of life. Music is then used to attain ethical perfection by inculcating these properties. In addition, it becomes the catharsis or purification of the soul, a vital psychical and physical force.[11]

Aristotle says that the amusement and relaxation is akin to sleep, drinking, and dancing which is sought for pleasure's sake (*Pol.* 1339a 15–20)[12]; and goes on to say that "music" administers to virtue by accustoming the player and hearer to rejoice rightly. There are nobler strains and meaner ones, sensual rhythms and rational rhythms, discord and harmony. The base soul delights in more primitive rhythms whereas great souls delight in harmonic order and gravity of theme (an opinion still held today by Bloom and others). Character or moral growth is abetted according to a diversity of "music's" delight, so that delight serves as a kind of practical middle term in the transition from "musical" values to moral formation. This is the second great finality of "music" for the Philosopher in that it accustoms us "to rejoice rightly" in various forms and noble imitations so that they may dispose us to act rightly as free and virtuous men.[13] Intellectual enjoyment is universally acknowledged to contain an element not only of the noble but of the pleasant, for happiness is made up of both; but we all pronounce "music" to be one of life's more pleasant experiences, and much to the philosopher's surprise with or without lyrics or melody (*Pol.* 1339a 16–20).

Aristotle also speaks of catharsis or purification or a "lightening" of the emotional state of a person as integral to experiencing good music. Rhythm is necessary to help in this process because it keeps the attention riveted on the melody and the words of a particular song. While pleasure in the arts can sometimes be excessive, especially for "musicians," yet these delights of music are meant ultimately to induce or entice people to the love of virtue. Human nature is inclined toward this experience since there is a natural love of imitation, which is why one of music's important purposes is ethical. "Music" is meant to be a mirror of virtue but unfortunately can become a focus of vice as well. Regarding the anti-music of Cage *et alii*, in his *Imaginary Landscape No. 4* (1951), twelve radios and twelve performers played at random. This was to become the new doctrine of "indeterminacy" in music, which has been spoken of as anti-music.[14] Given the popularity of so much music from rock to jazz, I would place him on the fringes (*pace* Grove's *Dictionary*) but he may have an influence on modern rock music in some ways. And while both Schoenberg and Stravinsky had some very strange things to say about music from the philosophical perspective, still in their later years, they produced some beautiful pieces. We need only remember that Schoenberg's work "Survivor from Warsaw" was performed for John Paul II on October 27, 1990, and Stravinsky wrote a Mass for the Catholic Cathedral of Santa Fe New Mexico in 1968.

Finally, we need to thank Mr. Reilly for calling to our attention some modern "classical" composers whose works are forged from a love of God, because when the work of the artist is linked to the glory of God, his art soars and radiates even more because he is in contact with infinite Beauty.

Basil Cole, O.P., a priest of the Most Holy Name of Jesus, Western Province of the Dominicans, is the author of *Music and Morals: A Theological Appraisal of the Moral and Psychological Effects of Music* (Alba House). He is co-author (with Paul Conner, O.P.) of *Christian Totality: A Theology of the Consecrated Life* (St. Paul Publications, Bombay). He has been a lecturer at the Pontifical University of St. Thomas in Rome.

Notes

1 Mary Louise Serafine, *Music As Cognition:The Development of Thought in Sound*, Columbia University Press, New York 1988, pp. 35–36.

2 Jacques Maritain, *Art and Scholasticism and the Frontiers of Poetry*, J. W. Evans (tr.), Scribner's, New York 1962, p. 125, n. 55.

3 In the *Laws* 812–813, Plato says that Greek poets should not have a " ... complexity and variation of notes. When the strings give one sound and the poet or composer of the melody gives another or less and greater intervals, slow and quick or high and low notes are combined. Opposite principles are confusing. Variety and complexity are apt to induce mental depression and confusion which might lead men away from the natural order of things into the realm of the irrational."

4 See the entry "Ethos" in *Grove's Dictionary of Music and Musicians,* Eric Blom (ed.), St. Martin's Press, New York 1956.

5 See "History of Music" and "Art of Music" in *NEB*; also, "Consonance" and a quotation from Guido of Arezzo under "Aesthetics of Music" in *New Grove Dictionary of Music and Musicians*.

6 Isobel Henderson, "Ancient Greek Music," in *Oxford History of Music*, H. E. Woolrede (ed.), revised Percy C. Bok (ed.) Oxford University Press, London 1929–38, vol I, p. 400.

7 R. P. Winnington-Ingram, *Mode in Ancient Greek Music*, Cambridge University Press, Cambridge, 1936.

8 John Hollander, *The Untuning of the Sky*, Princeton University Press, Princeton 1961, pp. 35–36.

9 James Anderson Winn, *Unsuspected Eloquence: A History of the Relations between Poetry and Music*, Yale University Press, New Haven 1981, p. 22. As a footnote to the history of music, it is to be noted that the myth surrounding the modes and their ethical effects gets into Ptolemy's *Harmonics* II, 7, and will influence many musicians and poets of the Renaissance.

10 See #112 of Iambilichus, *The Life of Pythagoras*, Gullian Clark (tr.), Liverpool University Press, Great Britain 1989. Here he asserts the legend of Pythagoras's ability to use music to stop murder and fornication by telling the musician to change the mode. Written by a Roman philosopher of mathematics in the third century, this little piece of information becomes part of the tradition through Boethius and onward.

11 Until the late thirteenth century, thirds and fourths were considered to be dissonant because of the Pythagorean tuning system. Only parallel fifths were considered to be consonant. Likewise, lutes and viols were tuned differently from keyboard instruments making a unified orchestra very difficult to exist. See *New Encyclopedia Britannica*,15th edition, Philip W. Goetz (ed.), Chicago 1986, "Music, Art of." See also *Oxford History of Music*, ed. by H. E. Woolrede, and revised ed. by Percy C. Bok, Vol, I, *The Polyphonic Period*, Oxford University, London 1929–38, where in chapter four, we find that by the ninth century, only parallel fifths were considered consonant harmony (cited in a work by Regino: *De Harmonica Institutione*). With regard to rhythm, in 1260, Franco of Cologne is the first to put time values to single notes and rests (see R. P. Winnington-Ingram, *Mode in Ancient Greek Music*, Cambridge University Press, Cambridge 1936.) he clearly shows that *harmoniae* and *tonoie* mean something quite different from harmony and tone in modern usage. The Greeks did not use scales in our sense of the word and *tonoi* were tunings of the *kithara* to be played.

12 In another context, he will call them the arts of play or the pleasurable arts (*Nic. Eth.* 116b, 35–37).

13 This is an inference of Dominic Rover, O.P., which Aristotle suggests but never quite comes to himself. See Rover's *The Poetics of Maritain: A Thomistic Critique*, The Thomist Press, Washington D. C. 1965, p. 83.

14 See Peter Yates, *Twentieth Century Music*, George Allen & Unwin, New York 1968, p. 28.

Chapter 10
The John Cardinal Wright Award
Acceptance Speech
September 29, 2001
Thomas W. Hilgers, M.D.

Words can truly not describe to all of you just how deeply grateful I am for being honored with this great award. If someone were to ask me how could one's work be best recognized, believe it or not, I think that I would respond to them by saying that to receive the recognition of the Fellowship of Catholic Scholars would truly be one of the highest forms of recognition I could possibly think of. I have always had a deep sense of the importance of Catholic scholarship, and the work that we have been doing is a dedication to that end.

Our work has been a research, scientific, educational, and clinical response to the challenges presented by Pope Paul VI in his truly great encyclical letter *Humanae Vitae*.[1] Not long ago I read Peter McGlory's book entitled *The Turning Point*, which was a defense of the work of the Papal Birth Control Commission. I found the book very interesting although completely wrong in its conclusions. The real "turning point" was *Humanae Vitae* itself. Just think for a moment what the world would be like if Pope Paul VI had adopted the position of the Papal Birth Control Commission! We would be hopelessly lost in a morass of genitocentric sexuality, without the hope of ever escaping its grasp.

In 1968, when *Humanae Vitae* was issued, I was a senior in medical school at the University of Minnesota. In going along with the times, I said to my fraternity brothers that I thought for sure the Church would change its position on contraception. Then, on July 25, 1968, Pope Paul VI issued *Humanae Vitae*. Having had an interest in these issues for many years, I went to the Newman Club chaplain at the University and asked where I could find a copy. His response to me was: "What do you want to read that kind of trash for?" Somehow, that seems to summarize the feelings of a lot of people at that time, although I did eventually find a copy and was able to read it.

In my reading of the encyclical, it didn't take me long to convert to the ways of *Humanae Vitae*. When I read in paragraph 9 about the characteristic marks and requirements of conjugal love, of which the Holy Father said, "It is of the greatest importance to have an exact understanding," I found that there would be no other conclusion except that reached by Paul VI. Just to briefly remind you of the content of paragraph 9 of the encyclical:

1. First of all, this love is human, and therefore both of the senses and of the spirit. For which reason, it is a product not only of natural instinct and inclinations; it also and primarily involves an act of free will. Through this act of free will [the spouses resolve] that their love will not only persevere through daily joys and sorrows but also increase. Therefore, it is especially important that they become one in heart and soul, and that they obtain together their human perfection.

2. Next, this love is total; that is, it is a very special form of personal friendship whereby the spouses generously share everything with each other without undue reservations and without concern for their selfish convenience. One who truly loves his spouse not only loves her for what he receives from her but also for her own sake. This he does joyfully, as he enriches [his beloved] with the gift of himself.

3. Furthermore, conjugal love is both *faithful* and exclusive to the end of life. Such, in fact, do the bride and groom conceive it to be on the day of their marriage, when they freely and consciously unite themselves by means of the marital bond. Even if fidelity at times presents difficulties, let no one deny that it is possible; rather, fidelity is always noble and of much merit. The example of many spouses throughout the ages has proved that fidelity is in accord with the very nature of marriage; even more, it has proved that intimate and lasting happiness flows from fidelity, just as from a fountain.

4. And finally, this love is *fruitful*, since the whole of the love is not contained in the communion of the spouses; it also looks beyond itself and seeks to raise up new lives. "Marriage and conjugal love are ordained by their very nature to the procreating and educating of children. Offspring are clearly the supreme gift of marriage, a gift that contributes immensely to the good of the parents themselves."

After reading this, especially the requirement of love to be total, it became quite clear to me where the Church would come out on this issue and why. How could one love another totally while saying to them: "I love you for all that you are except for your fertility." It has only been made complicated by those who are unwilling to accept the total love that should exist within marriage. This encyclical letter is an extraordinary expression of love from the Church to its members.

The most difficult part of Humanae Vitae is found in Part III, the Pastoral Directives. In this section, the Church calls upon public authorities, men of science, Christian spouses, the apostolate of spouses, doctors and health care professionals, priests, and bishops to fulfill their responsibilities in seeing to it that this teaching is activated. It was in reading these, with special reference to the appeal to "men of science" and "doctors and health care professionals" that, in December,1968, I began my first research experiment in the area of the natural regulation of human fertility.

Since that time, so much has happened. In 1976, as a young faculty member in the Department of Obstetrics and Gynecology at St. Louis University School of Medicine, I began to direct a team of research investigators whose goal was to conduct an independent evaluation of the Billings Ovulation Method of natural family planning. At the beginning of this research, we all fully anticipated that this work would eventually lead to a better understanding of the natural methods for the regulation of human fertility. In fact, that has been accomplished. However, we ended up accomplishing much more than we could have ever predicted.

After spending 11 years in academic medicine at St. Louis University and Creighton University School of Medicine, I left a fully tenured professorship to start, along with my wife, the Pope Paul VI Institute for the Study of Human Reproduction. Our commitment to build this Institute was made on the day that Pope Paul

VI died, August 6, 1978. Having grown to deeply appreciate the teaching presented in *Humanae Vitae* during his pontificate, we both had a deep desire to respond to these pastoral directives; and our commitment to build this Institute was a direct response to Paul VI's invitation to become more involved in becoming a part of the solution. On that very day, we dedicated ourselves to building a living memorial, in research, education and service, as a direct response to the call presented to us by Pope Paul VI.

Shortly after we began our work, we literally stumbled upon a standardization of the Billings Method. This standardized modification of the Billings Method has now become known as the Creighton Model Fertility*Care*™ System. Our ability to use it as a means of both achieving and avoiding a pregnancy while at the same time having a system that could vastly improve women's health, is a direct result of this standardization.

In 1978, we began the first allied health professional education program for Fertility*Care* Practitioners (at the time called Natural Family Planning Practitioners). This fall, we will embark upon our 24th consecutive year of training Fertility*Care* Practitioners, Instructors, Supervisors, Educators, and Medical Consultants. In addition, we have recently added Physician Assistants, Nurse Practitioners, Pharmacists and Nurse Midwives to our training program. In addition, we conduct a Catholic Leadership Conference twice a year for priests, religious, and lay leaders in the Church.

Over these past 24 years, we have trained well over 1000 teachers of this system. We have established 132 Fertility*Care* Centers in the United States and this number is growing daily. We have others in at least 10 foreign countries. In addition, we are training approximately 30 physicians per year. The latter we view as an extraordinary accomplishment because when we first began this effort, it was nearly impossible to attract physicians to it. The more recent development of the new medical and surgical women's health science of NaProTECHNOLOGY® forms the foundation upon which the interest amongst physician is increasing.

In September 1985, we were able to open the doors of the Pope Paul VI Institute. We did this out of a complete act of faith! While it has been an extraordinarily difficult struggle to find the resources to continue this effort, we are now in our 16th year of operation and we have far exceeded our ability to imagine what could be accomplished.

In 1991, the real crown jewel of the Institute was first described. This was a new reproductive science called NaProTECHNOLOGY® which was introduced in a small textbook entitled *The Medical Applications of Natural Family Planning*. It is this textbook that we have been using for the last ten years. At the same time, the evaluation of our research efforts has grown enormously during this period of time and we are in the final stages of preparing a major new medical textbook to be entitled *The Medical and Surgical Practice of NaProTECHNOLOGY®* which actually will be the first definitive presentation of this new science. This will present all of the scientific foundations and practice principles of this new approach that is completely consistent with Catholic teaching.

In reality, we have been privileged to study women and married couples at the stages of procreation that exist prior to, during the time of and following conception. We have been privileged to observe women's health both from the traditional perspective as well as from the new perspective of the Creighton Model Fertility*Care*™ System and NaProTECHNOLOGY®. We have been able to implement strategies that have improved our ability to evaluate the medical problems that might exist and subsequently to treat them.

In this new textbook, we will be outlining the effects of treatment of recurrent ovarian cysts, abnormal bleeding, premenstrual syndrome, a variety of hormonal deficiencies that exist during the course of the menstrual and fertility cycles, and of women who have infertility and repetitive miscarriage and other reproductive abnormalities. We will show that the success rates that we have had by applying this new science exceed by a significant margin the current success rates of the artificial reproductive technologies. In addition, we have previously shown that the Creighton Model Fertility*Care*™ System is already equal to or superior in effectiveness to oral contraceptives.

In our efforts, we have been dedicated to conducting this work completely within the context of Catholic teaching. That has been our guidepost and our beacon. We have done this without shame. We have progressed boldly though at times with great difficulty because the contemporary society still does not understand what the Church is trying to say.

My wife likes to say that over the last 25 years we have been "field testing" the teachings of the Church, and over these same 25 years we have more and more found how successful they can be to real people. While the Church is often ridiculed for her position on contraception, sterilization, abortion, and *in vitro* fertilization (and other artificial reproductive technologies), we have shown that these teachings are superior to those artificial and destructive approaches. At the same time, our method maintains the moral integrity of one's decision making, the dignity of the human person, and the integrity of marriage and the family. We have no doubt that this will find its proper place within humankind; and that it will increase a human person's ability to love and be loved, to share and to serve, to evangelize in a world that hurts deeply, and, finally, to love in ways that we have not been able to do in the past. We thank the Church for her leadership over these centuries and millennia. We hope that in some small way this work will help bolster the confidence that the Church and society might have in these remarkable teachings. And I thank the Fellowship of Catholic Scholars for their willingness to recognize these efforts. Thank you very much

Thomas W. Hilgers, M.D., is the founder and director of the Pope Paul VI Institute for the Study of Human Reproduction in Omaha, Nebraska, where he currently serves as Senior Medical Consultant in Obstetrics, Gynecology, Reproduction Medicine and Surgery. He is also a member of the prestigious Society of Reproductive Surgeons.

Dr. Hilgers founded and directed the Creighton University Natural Family Planning Education and Research Center. Along with his colleagues, he is the developer of the Creighton Model Fertility*Care*™ System, a thoroughly standardized modification of the Billings' Ovulation Method. His on-going medical research and the application of this method have led to the development of the new gynecological and reproductive science called NaProTECHNOLOGY.

An accomplished author, he is the recipient of four different research awards and several honorary doctorates. In 1997, the Nebraska Family Council named Dr. Hilgers Physician of the Year. He and his wife Susan are the parents of four sons and a daughter.

Notes

1 Pope Paul VI, encyclical letter *Humanae Vitae: A Challenge to Love.* Introductory Essay and New Translation by Janet E. Smith, Ph.D. New Hope, Kentucky 40052.

SPECIAL CONVENTION SESSION

Chapter 11
A New Era in the Renewal of the Liturgy: The Holy See Issues Its "Fifth Instruction" Implementing the Vatican II Liturgical Reforms
Helen Hull Hitchcock

Liturgiam Authenticam

A major document on liturgical translation was made public by the Holy See at a press conference held at the Vatican May 7, 2001. *Liturgiam Authenticam* (Authentic Liturgy), *On the Use of Vernacular Languages in the Publication of the Books of the Roman Liturgy*, is the Fifth Instruction on the implementation of the Second Vatican Council's liturgical reforms in the nearly 40 years since the Council and one with far-reaching implications for Catholic worship.

This high-level document, issued by the Congregation for Divine Worship and the Discipline of the Sacraments, was expressly approved by Pope John Paul II and became effective April 25, 2001. It appeared on the Vatican web site the same afternoon. In process for about three years, *Liturgiam Authenticam* appeared in time to provide translation norms for the new third *editio typica*, or "typical edition," of the Roman Missal, the Latin version of which is expected to be released soon. It also arrives near the end of a massive project of re-translation and revision of the major liturgical books used by the Catholic Church in English-speaking countries that began more than 10 years ago.

In the light of this authoritative new document that "seeks to prepare for a new era of liturgical renewal," further amendment of the revised books already submitted to the Holy See and still awaiting approval will apparently be required. The Instruction calls for correcting existing vernacular translations:

> The omissions or errors which affect certain existing vernacular translations...have impeded the progress of the inculturation that actually should have taken place. In fact,

it seems necessary to consider anew the true notion of liturgical translation in order that the translations of the Sacred Liturgy into the vernacular languages may stand secure as the authentic voice of the Church of God (§7).

The Instruction's five chapters cover: 1) the choice of vernacular languages for liturgical use; 2) principles of translation (including norms for Scripture translations for Lectionaries and sung texts); 3) procedures for preparing translations and the establishment of commissions (e.g., "mixed" commissions, such as the International Commission on English in the Liturgy (ICEL), which produced most of the English-language liturgical texts now in use); 4) detailed publication procedures; and 5) the translation of "proper" texts for feasts and observances special to some territories and religious orders.

The new Instruction provides concrete rules for "preparing all translations of the liturgical books." It explicitly replaces all other norms that have been used for this purpose except the Fourth Instruction, *Varietates Legitimae* (on inculturation), issued in 1994. However, *Liturgiam Authenticam* incorporates much of the Congregation for the Doctrine of the Faith's 1997 interim "Norms for the Translation of Biblical Texts for Use in the Liturgy," and goes even further in one particular:

> The term 'fathers', found in many biblical passages and liturgical texts of ecclesiastical composition, is to be rendered by the corresponding masculine word into vernacular languages insofar as it may be seen to refer to the patriarchs or the kings of the chosen people in the Old Testament, or to the fathers of the Church (§31).

No "Inclusivisms"

Liturgiam Authenticam emphasizes that liturgical translation must be "exact in wording and free from all ideological influence." Translation is not to be "creative innovation"; its fundamental purpose is to render "the original texts faithfully and accurately into the vernacular language...without paraphrases or glosses." The words of Sacred Scripture and the liturgical texts, the Instruction says, "are not intended primarily to be a sort of mirror of the interior dispositions of the faithful; rather they express truths that transcend the limits of time and space."

Thus, the translation must not be time-bound or limited by any political, ideological or theological theories of the translators. Although the document never directly mentions so-called "inclusive language," a feminist-driven attempt to neuter English that has plagued virtually every other Christian ecclesial body in the English-speaking world, and has affected almost all Scripture and liturgical translations since the mid-1970s, there is no ambiguity about the matter in the new Instruction:

> When the original text, for example, employs a single term in expressing the interplay between the individual and the universality and unity of the human family or community (such as the Hebrew word '*adam*, the Greek *anthropos*, or the Latin *homo*), this property of the language of the original text should be maintained in the translation (§30).

In other words, the standard English generic words, "man," and "mankind," are to be retained in English liturgical translations. This is in marked contrast to the US bishops' 1990 *Criteria for the Evaluation of Inclusive Language Translations of Scriptural Texts Proposed for Liturgical Use*, which had proposed "person," "people," or "human family" be used in translating these same words.

Sacral Vocabulary Restored

Liturgiam Authenticam, however, never mentions these inclusivist *Criteria,* nor does it mention a 1969 statement on translation by the Consilium (the commission that coordinated liturgical changes in the years immediately following the Council). Known by its French title, *Comme le prévoit* ("as foreseen"), this set of translation principles promoted replacing words and concepts of the original text with vernacular terms deemed more "relevant"; it rejected customary sacral language; it advocated "adaptations" and altering metaphors to appeal to the taste of the times. For example, it asserted:

> Many of the phrases of approach to the Almighty were originally adapted from forms of address to the sovereign in the courts of Byzantium and Rome. It is necessary to study how far an attempt should be made to offer equivalents in modern English for such words as "*quaesumus*," "*dignare*," "*clementissime*," "*maiestas*," and the like (§13 d) – "we

beseech," "to be considered worthy," "most merciful," "majesty."

According to *Comme le prévoit:*

> It is not sufficient that a formula handed down from some other time or region be translated verbatim, even if accurately, for liturgical use. The formula translated must become the genuine prayer of the congregation and in it each of its members should be able to find and express himself or herself (§20c).

By contrast, the new Instruction *Liturgiam Authenticam* sees great importance in a specifically sacral vocabulary:

> While the translation must transmit the perennial treasury of orations by means of language understandable in the cultural context for which it is intended, it should also be guided by the conviction that liturgical prayer not only is formed by the genius of a culture, but itself contributes to the development of that culture. Consequently it should cause no surprise that such language differs somewhat from ordinary speech. Liturgical translation...will facilitate the development of a sacral vernacular, characterized by a vocabulary, syntax and grammar that are proper to divine worship...(§47).

> Since the liturgical books of the Roman Rite contain many fundamental words of the theological and spiritual tradition of the Roman Church, every effort must be made to preserve this system of vocabulary rather than substituting other words...(§50).

> [A] deficiency in translating the varying forms of addressing God, such as *Domine, Deus, Omnipotens aeterne Deus, Pater,* and so forth, as well as the various words expressing supplication, may render the translation monotonous and obscure the rich and beautiful way in which the relationship between the faithful and God is expressed in the Latin text. (§51).

This focus on fidelity first and foremost in *Liturgiam Authenticam,* even in cases where unfamiliar terms and "ambiguities" may need explanation, is a very sharp departure from the prevailing theories of liturgical translators in recent decades, and also from earlier translation guidelines in use. However, it recognizes the principle enunciated in the Second Vatican Council's Constitution on the Liturgy and elsewhere that liturgical change should be "organic," and should develop gradually while retaining the integrity of the Church's history and heritage, rather than be forced to conform to the "spirit of the age."

Role of Holy See in Translation Strengthened

Another significant departure in the Instruction from practices in recent decades is that all liturgical texts and all changes proposed must receive a *recognitio*, or approval, by the Holy See (i.e., by the Congregation for Divine Worship and the Discipline of the Sacraments) before they may be published or used. This assures "the authenticity of the translation and its correspondence with the original texts," the Instruction says, and explains further:

> This practice both expresses and effects a bond of communion between the successor of blessed Peter and his brothers in the Episcopate. Furthermore, this *recognitio* is not a mere formality, but is rather an exercise of the power of governance, which is absolutely necessary (in the absence of which the act of the Conference of Bishops in no way attains legal force); and modifications, even substantial ones, may be introduced by means of it. For this reason it is not permissible to publish, for the use of celebrants or for the general public, any liturgical texts that have been translated or recently composed, as long as the recognitio is lacking (§80).

Even the translators employed by the "mixed commissions" are now to be approved by the CDW (§102). The rationale for this is given as follows:

> It is necessary to uphold the principle according to which each particular Church must be in accord with the universal Church not only as regards the doctrine of the Faith and the sacramental signs, but also as regards those practices universally received through apostolic and continuous tradition. For these reasons, the required *recognitio* of the Apostolic See is intended to ensure that the translations themselves, as well as any variations introduced into them, will not harm the unity of God's people, but will serve it instead (§80).

In other words, there will be no more "original texts" composed by translators. The "mixed" commissions are to limit themselves to the translation of the *editiones typicae*, leaving aside all theoretical questions not directly related to this work, and not involving themselves either in relations with other "mixed" commissions or in the composition of original texts (98).

"I Believe..."

Among the changes that most Catholics may notice first is the Instruction's explicit requirement that the Creed, *Credo* ("I believe") be translated accurately (§ 65, 74). For thirty years, English-speaking Catholics have said "we believe". The Instruction explains:

> The Creed is to be translated according to the precise wording that the tradition of the Latin Church has bestowed upon it, including the use of the first person singular, by which is clearly made manifest that the confession of faith is handed down in the Creed, as it were, as coming from the person of the whole Church, united by means of the Faith.

"And with your spirit" also returns. The current English translation, of course, renders *et cum spiritu tuo as* "and also with you." The phrase *mea culpa, mea culpa, mea maxima culpa* will once again be "through my fault, through my fault, through my most grievous fault"; it is currently translated "through my own fault"(§56, 65). As the Instruction notes:

> Certain expressions that belong to the heritage of the whole or of a great part of the ancient Church, as well as others that have become part of the general human patrimony, are to be respected by a translation that is as literal as possible, as for example the words of the people's response *Et cum spiritu tuo*, or the expression *mea culpa, mea culpa, mea maxima culpa* in the Act of Penance of the Order of Mass.

"Yahweh" Will Disappear

> In accordance with immemorial tradition, which indeed is already evident in the above-mentioned "Septuagint" version, the name of almighty God expressed by the Hebrew tetragrammaton (YHWH) and rendered in Latin by the word *Dominus*, is to be rendered into any given vernacular by a word equivalent in meaning (§41c).

The Instruction also states that texts "which the faithful will have committed to memory" should not be changed notably "without real necessity"; and when changes are necessary, they should be made "at one time" and be explained to people (§64, 74).

Sung Texts

The Instruction includes brief but important paragraphs on music. Liturgical texts that are sung are to be faithful first of all to the text: "Paraphrases are not to be substituted with the intention of making them more easily set to music, nor may hymns considered generically equivalent be employed in their place" (§60). This implies that the practices of substituting refrains from songs for the prescribed Memorial Acclamations or supplanting sung texts like the *Agnus Dei* ("Lamb of God") with new phrases will have to cease.

"A New Period Begins"

The document concludes with directions to national bishops' conferences:

> [F]rom the day on which this Instruction is published, a new period begins for the making of emendations or for undertaking anew the consideration of the introduction of vernacular languages or idioms into liturgical use, as well as for revising translations heretofore made into vernacular languages (§131).

An "integral plan" for revising the vernacular translations of liturgical books translated is to be submitted to the Congregation for Divine Worship "within five years from the date of publication of this Instruction" by the Presidents of the Conferences of Bishops and the heads of religious houses. The norms of this Instruction "attain full force for the emendation of previous translations, and any further delay in making such emendations is to be avoided".

Helen Hull Hitchcock is the editor of the *Adoremus Bulletin*, the monthly publication of the Society for the Renewal of the Sacred Liturgy, under whose auspices the above talk was first prepared and sent to news media on May 7, 2001; it appeared that same day on the *Adoremus* website and was subsequently published in the June, 2001, issue of the *Adoremus Bulletin*. Mrs. Hitchcock also edited the influential volume *The Politics of Prayer: Feminist Language and the Worship of God* (San Francisco: Ignatius Press, 1992), which helped launch the on-going movement for "the reform of the reform" in liturgy.

The versatile Mrs. Hitchcock is also one of the founders and is currently the President of Women for Faith and Family (WFF), and principal author of WFF's "Affirmation for Catholic Women." She also edits WFF's publication *Voices*. She is married to St. Louis University history professor James Hitchcock, the well-known Catholic writer and columnist, and a past President of the Fellowship of Catholic Scholars, as well as the third recipient of the FCS Cardinal Wright Award. The Hitchcocks are the parents of four adult daughters.

Chapter 12
Liturgiam Authenticam and the Prospects for Authenitc Liturgical Renewal
Rev. Jerry Pokorsky

With the release of *Liturgiam Authenticam* (LA) in the spring of 2001, the Vatican has signaled its steady resolve to save the Roman Rite. There can be no mistake that this Instruction on Liturgical Translation can not only be numbered among the highly authoritative Vatican documents; it also reveals the Church's determination to ensure accurate translations for the Roman Rite. But how will this new Vatican Instruction be received by the Church in English-speaking countries? What effect will it have on the new ICEL[1] Sacramentary, ICEL's massive translation project of the Roman Missal?

For those who have been promoting accurate and theologically sound translations of the Roman Missal, the Instruction was received with a good deal of satisfaction. One observer who studied the new Instruction made these comments (edited slightly for inclusion here) in e-mail correspondence:

> The witch is dead. LA's treatment of the inclusivist project (30) is both subtle and forceful. It carefully steers clear of conceding even the existence of "inclusive language" and "exclusive language," as linguistic realities, but rightly emphasizes that it is the duty of catechists and homilists – not translators – to ensure that ambiguous words are understood in their naturally, inherently inclusive sense. The Holy See refuses to concede that natural language, including the natural language employed by the sacred authors and in the liturgy, is "sexist." NB: it's not a question of "balance," or of "moderate inclusive language," or of "horizontal inclusive language," or of

concession to historicism ("they were sexists back then, but we should preserve the sexism of the originals anyway"). The notion that language "encodes" prejudice wins no recognition whatsoever. Nor does the Holy See concede that bigotry exists on the surface reading: "Similarly, it is the task of catechists or of the homilist to transmit that right interpretation of the texts that excludes any prejudice or unjust discrimination on the basis of persons, gender, social condition, race or other criteria, which has no foundation at all in the texts of the Sacred Liturgy" (29).

There are a number of significant restorations:
• The Latin texts to be translated into the vernacular "are themselves the fruit of the liturgical renewal" (20) and are declared not to be in need of a second order "renewal" by liturgists and translators. In other words, the task of the mixed commissions is accurate translation – not the correction, not the updating, and not the "improvement" of the Latin text!
• "I believe" wins over "We believe" by straight knockout: "The Creed is to be translated according to the precise wording that the tradition of the Latin Church has bestowed upon it, including the use of the first person singular, by which is clearly made manifest that 'the confession of faith is handed down in the Creed, as it were, as coming from the person of the whole Church, united by means of the Faith'" (65).
• The National Conference of Catholic Bishops' (NCCB) 1990 inclusivist "Translation Norms" are now "history": "When the original text, for example, employs a single term in expressing the interplay between the individual and the universality and unity of the human family or community (such as the Hebrew word 'adam, the Greek anthropos, or the Latin homo), this property of the language of the original text should be maintained in the translation." (30). Further, "to be avoided is the systematic resort to imprudent solutions such as a mechanical substitution of words, the transition from the singular to the plural, the splitting of a unitary collective term into masculine and feminine parts, or the introduction of impersonal or abstract words" (31). This means that the new politically correct Bible translations, such as the New Revised Standard Version

(NRSV) and the Revised New American Bible (RNAB), along with much of the new Lectionary, and, of course, every ICEL production since 1975 have now been or will be torpedoed.

• LA makes its own the pertinent CDF "Norms for the Translation of Biblical Texts for Use in the Liturgy" (31), and even goes further in one particular: "The term 'Fathers', found in many biblical passages and liturgical texts of ecclesiastical composition, is to be rendered by the corresponding masculine word into vernacular languages insofar as it may be seen to refer to the patriarchs or the kings of the chosen people in the Old Testament, or to the Fathers of the Church."

• "And with your spirit" is back: "Certain expressions that belong to the heritage of the whole or of a great part of the ancient Church, as well as others that have become part of the general human patrimony, are to be respected by a translation that is as literal as possible, as for example the words of the people's response *Et cum spiritu tuo*, or the expression *mea culpa, mea culpa, mea maxima culpa* in the Act of Penance of the Order of Mass."

• Good-bye to "alternative collects," and the like. "The 'mixed' commissions are to limit themselves to the translation of the *editiones typicae*, leaving aside all theoretical questions not directly related to this work, and not involving themselves either in relations with other "mixed" commissions or in the composition of original texts" (98).

Delight with the document is not universal, however. Bishop Donald W. Trautman of Erie, Pennsylvania, has been vocal in protesting against the document in several publications. As the Chairman of the Bishops' Committee on Liturgy when the ICEL Sacramentary was being debated by the American bishops, Bishop Trautman was also a leading proponent of this ICEL Sacrmentary. But his view is apparently shared by only a few bishops.

Liturgiam Authenticam is the Fifth Instruction for the right implementation of the Constitution on the Sacred Liturgy of the Second Vatican Council. The Pope personally approved it for release and promulgation.[2] The new Instruction thus has considerable more authority than the 1969 Vatican document called *Comme le prévoit* ("As foreseen"), frequently invoked by ICEL to justify its translation practices: "The norms set forth in this Instruction are to be substituted for all norms previously published on the matter, with the exception of the Instruction *Varietates legitimae"* (8). The latter Instruction has to do with liturgical inculturation and was issued by the Vatican in 1994.

ICEL's so-called "dynamic equivalent" method of translation can be traced to *Comme le prévoit.* So, for example, in the *Confiteor,* the Latin *"mea culpa, mea culpa, mea maxima culpa"* ("through my fault, through my fault, through my most grievous fault") continued to be mistranslated by ICEL because it was claimed that repetition is tedious in English. So the phrase was translated simply as "through my fault." There are many such examples of ICEL's mistranslation of the Latin texts of the Mass.

Even as the bishops wearily approved the ICEL texts after extended debates in the 1990s, the Vatican was sending signals that the ICEL translation principles were outdated. In January and February 1994, a delegation from the NCCB, including bishops working on Scripture translations for the Lectionary, and a panel of scholars appointed by the Holy See, met to discuss the problems with translations of Scripture texts involving so-called "inclusive language" and other issues. Subsequently it was revealed that the Vatican had issued norms for translation to govern translations of Scripture texts proposed for liturgical use. However, these norms, in large part now ratified in *Liturgiam Authenticam,* were not revealed to the body of bishops until 1997.

On June 20, 1996, Archbishop Geraldo Majella Agnelo of the CDW said the Vatican was aware of the pointed debate over liturgical translations, but said the Holy See "pays more attention to the results that are ultimately approved by the bishops' conferences." Archbishop Agnelo also offered a clarification about the 1969 Vatican Instruction on Liturgical Translation *Comme le prévoit.* He said that while *Comme le prévoit* contains "valuable principles," it must be recognized "as a text dated 1969, from the first period of liturgical reform." He said that its current value "is therefore conditioned by the experience of the last 27 years, along with the fact that there exist new canon law norms regarding the approval of such translations."

A year later, in 1997, in a letter to Bishop Anthony M. Pilla, President of the National Conference of Catholic Bishops, then Archbishop Jorge Medina Estévez, Pro-Prefect of the Congregation for Divine Worship and the Discipline of the Sacraments said that

ICEL's translation of the Ordination Ritual would not be confirmed "not only by reason of its failure to adhere faithfully to the Latin *editio typica altera* and to convey accurately in English its contents, but also because the translation is not without doctrinal problems." Archbishop Medina observed that because "the shortcomings are so diffused...minor isolated corrections will not suffice." (The revised Ordination Ritual of bishops, priests and deacons (*De Ordinatione Episcopi, Presbyterorum et Diaconorum*) had been approved by the Administrative Committee of the NCCB in March 1996.)

All of the problems identified in Archbishop Medina's letter would also apply to the new translation of the ICEL Sacramentary, and would prefigure the translation principles that would be enunciated by *Liturgiam Authenticam*:

• "...the translation is seriously deficient. Particularly problematic are the texts that form part of the Eucharistic Prayer..."

• "Prominent among the problems is the decision of the translators to break with common Catholic usage and translate the Latin '*presbyteri*' into English not with 'priests' but with 'presbyters.'"

• "[The translation] fails to transmit faithfully important doctrinal aspects of the Latin original."

• "It is also a cause for concern that the translators have felt free to introduce changes at will, to 'improve' the order of the text, the rubrics, and the numbering."

• "To the above-mentioned translation have been added new compositions. These have been found to be in disharmony with the conventions of the Roman Liturgy, confused, largely unsuited to the circumstances in which they would be used, and at best theologically impoverished."

• "...the Second Eucharistic Prayer which in Latin runs '*una cum Papa nostro* N. *et Episcopo nostro* N. *et universo clero*' [was translated] 'together with N. our Pope, N. our bishop, and all the ministers of your Gospel'. This was found unacceptable by the Bishops' Conference of the United States of America and by the Holy See. It could reasonably have been expected that the translators would thereafter take note that translations of that kind were not acceptable. This did not in fact happen, however. In n. 59 of this proposed translation we find '*universo clero*' now rendered by 'all who are called to your service', an even wider expression."

Hence, by late 2001, it was not surprising that the ICEL Sacramentary continued to languish in the Vatican without Vatican confirmation. In retrospect, it is clear that *Liturgiam Authenticam* in fact consolidated a half-decade of intense Vatican involvement in the English-speaking translation enterprise. It is also clear that the resistance of the liturgical establishment to Vatican guidance has gravely hampered authentic renewal of the liturgy.

The present Bishops' Committee on Liturgy has a new staff that appears to be cooperating with the Vatican dicasteries. During the last week of November 2001, there was a Catholic News Service article that quoted Father James Moroney, the executive director of the Bishops' Committee on Liturgy, as saying that the ICEL Sacramentary will never be approved – which suggests that the problems with ICEL's translation are insurmountable.

Conclusion

In 1968, Pope Paul VI released the encyclical *Humanae Vitae*. Against all odds, humanly speaking, *Humanae Vitae* reaffirmed the Church's central teaching on the dignity of marriage and the evil of contraception. When *Liturgiam Authenticam* was released 33 years later, it was received with a similar surprise, joy and resentment that greeted *Humanae Vitae*, although on a far smaller scale. But there are parallels. Just as the teachings of *Humanae Vitae* reaffirm the authentic nature of human sexuality, *Liturgiam Authenticam* reaffirms eminently reasonable liturgical translation principles.

Like *Humanae Vitae, Liturgiam Authenticam* affirms the normal. But the passion for resistance lies not so much with the average Catholic, but with an entrenched liturgical establishment. Because the majority of grass-roots practicing Catholics are either passionately in favor of faithful translations, or at worst indifferent, there is reason for optimism. Still, it is not clear whether the Vatican's principles of translation will be implemented without serious obstacles over the next few years. Pope John Paul II is in the twilight years of his pontificate. Cardinal Medina of the CDW, the hero of faithful liturgical translations, is close to retirement. Still, it would be unusual for a new pope to modify or reverse an Instruction having such a high level of authority.

There are more immediate concerns. The liturgical establishment continues to control an immense liturgical publishing empire that is quite capable of undermining the most profound and beautiful of Vatican documents. It is easy to imagine a refusal to follow Vatican instructions. But one thing is certain. Just as *Humanae Vitae* serves as a continuing indictment of an unnatural contraceptive culture, so the highly authoritative directives of *Liturgiam Authenticam* will serve as a continuing indictment of inherently bad translations, should they recur. If only to this extent, Catholics who are praying for accurate and beautiful liturgical translations have good reason for hope.

Rev. Jerry Pokorsky is a priest of the diocese of Arlington, Virginia, where he is currently serving as the administrator of the mission church of St. Peter in Washington, Virginia. He was one of the founders of the Credo organization of priests that was influential in promoting more accurate liturgical translations from the Latin in the period before *Liturgiam Authenticam* was issued. He edits Credo's newsletter and is also a member of the Executive Committee (with Rev. Joseph Fessio, S.J., and Helen Hull Hitchcock) of the Society for the Renewal of the Sacred Liturgy, which publishes the *Adoremus Bulletin*, in which Fr. Pokorsky's articles frequently appear, as they do in such publications as *The Catholic World Report*.

Notes

1   ICEL (The International Commission on English in the Liturgy) was established on October 17, 1963, as an unincorporated association of bishops. In 1967, ICEL was incorporated in Canada. The founding bishops represented the following conferences: Australia, Canada, England and Wales, India, Ireland, New Zealand, Pakistan, Scotland, South Africa, and the United States. An eleventh "member" conference, The Philippines, joined ICEL in 1967. Each member conference appoints a bishop representative to the Episcopal Board of ICEL. In subsequent years fifteen other conferences were added as "associate members." They include: The Antilles, Bangladesh, Cepac (Fiji Islands, Raratonga, Samoa and Tokelau, Tonga), Gambia-Liberia-Sierra Leone, Ghana,

Kenya, Malaysia-Singapore, Malawi, Nigeria, Papua New Guinea and the Solomons, Sri Lanka, Tanzania, Uganda, Zambia, Zimbabwe. In 1995, ICEL revenues were $767,976, most of which came from royalty revenue of $601,477 and Conference of Bishops assessments of $155,427. (International Commission on English in the Liturgy, 1522 K Street, Suite 1000, Washington, DC 20005-1202 U.S.A.)

2   The Instruction was prepared by the Congregation for Divine Worship and the Discipline of the Sacraments (CDW). Pope John Paul II approved this Instruction and confirmed it by his own authority in an audience granted to the Cardinal Secretary of State on March 20, 2001.

Chapter 13
When Beauty Is Revolutionary:
Reflections on *Liturgiam Authenticam*
Father Raymond T. Gawronski, SJ

The Word has power a power to penetrate and transform the darkness of matter without being itself destroyed (John 1). The words of Christ have been known to tumble empires.[1] "What doth it profit a man to gain the whole world and lose his soul." Those words once changed the direction of my young life, and have haunted me ever since.

The other day, I tried to make sense of a Gospel reading – a sense that had somehow been lost in translation, slipping through the mind that yet balked at its unfamiliar cadence: "I have come to call, not the self-righteous, but sinners" (Matt. 9:13 Lectionary [1970] Feast of Saint Matthew, September 21).

As I read this, I knew something was wrong: the words did not flow. One stumbles over "self-righteous" – even if it *were* a literal translation of the text, which it is not. In fact, this translation turns the very words of Jesus upside down and ignores the tradition, *Felix culpa*! (happy fault). For His point seems to be that those who are, in fact, *righteous* are not in need of Him. The *self*-righteous would be sinners.

Ideologies are political systems for the mind, clung to by people like the Pharisees who cannot venture into the bracing world of ideas on their own. Because it is not grounded in truth, or goodness, or beauty, but rather in the shifting sands of worldly power, ideology has a way of creating ugliness. (Much of our modern church architecture has been described as an "ideology in stone.")

Ugliness can also infect language. It can be heard in the Sequence for Our Lady of Sorrows as it appears in the Lectionary (1970).

"Virgin of all virgins blest!
Listen to my fond request:
Let me share your grief divine.

Let me to my latest breath,
In my body bear the death
Of that dying Son of yours."

That Son of *yours*? Anything, anything, to avoid the word "thine" which, though it fits beautifully into the rhyme of the hymn, is so redolent of that old world that it must yield to the linguistic bulldozer. That Son of *yours*. Our Lord God, demeaned for ideological reasons, not for the first time in the twentieth century, but now by the Church?

The 1960s were a heady time in the world, and, with *Liturgiam Authenticam*, the Church is finally, it seems, coming to terms with the most gratuitous wrong turns that came about at that time and subsequently set the course for Catholic worship. Thus, I would like to share some reflections on the document and some of its effects.

Vatican II offered a tremendous invitation to the Church worldwide: to a new collegiality, and with it, a new responsibility. It was perhaps natural, but sad for all that, that local churches, at least the ones in our English-speaking purview, should so quickly have been commandeered by groups with ideological axes to grind. It is commonly acknowledged that people with well-formed agendas moved into the power vacuum created by the turn from Trent.

Revolutions are famous for spawning committees. After the Council, rather than accepting the responsibility that adulthood should bring, some Catholics continued playing rebellious games with the "powers that be" trying to get away with as much as they could, taunting, teasing authority to step in and do something about it, always with an eye on the all-policing media.

The Spirit of the 1960s

The 1969 document *Comme le prévoit* ("as foreseen") served for several decades as the standard for translating liturgical documents. Its very title – in the vernacular – speaks of the spirit of the 1960s that produced it. In the world that "spirit" had some things to commend it; in the Church it has proven disastrous insofar as that which claimed to be a spirit of *liberation* (fundamentally a critique) came to serve as the basis for forming a new canon, setting a new standard for developing liturgy and liturgical translation within the Church.

At the heart of what the spirit of the 1960s meant for the Church was an identification of the Church's best intentions with the agendas of elites in the political and academic worlds. There had to be a cadre who could adequately read the "signs of the times," who could professionally interpret the *Zeitgeist* for the retrograde religious mind now lost and confused in the "Secular City."

Perhaps the central item taken into the Church from the intellectual world of the 1960s was the self-hatred of a certain type of European intellectual. Ignoring the experience of the Eastern half of Europe at any time, past or present – that is, discounting the ongoing experience of modern totalitarianism – these intellectuals were true children of Rousseau, seeking paradise anywhere but in their own European civilization. And who more fully represented that civilization than Rome and the Roman Church?

Rejecting all that was past, the Red Guards of China or the New Left of Europe and America were determined to smash all that had been in order that heaven might finally be realized on earth. Key to this was the vision of a "noble savage," unfettered by the burden of history, tradition, or the constriction of classical form. The "noble savage" could be found anywhere at all except in traditional culture – and nobility could only be found in the savage. Tradition was seen as basically constrictive and oppressive.

Recovery of the "Roman Tradition"

Perhaps the most important thing to be said about *Liturgiam Authenticam* is that it reasserts the dignity of the Roman tradition within the Catholic Church: it insists that the Roman tradition is a tradition worthy of respect, indeed, one that serves as the standard for the further development of that religious tradition, even as the Eastern traditions are for the Eastern Churches.

For years, a campaign has been waged against any sort of "Latinization" in the Eastern Churches. Though I suspect that that has at times been overdone in the Christian East, there is much to commend a concern for purity of tradition.

This cultural purism, however, has strangely been ignored in the Latin Church, marginalized along with the so-called "traditionalists." *Liturgiam Authenticam* finally says something that Eastern

Catholics have been saying for decades: there is an authentic tradition here, with its own dignity and riches. And this authentic tradition must be central in the ongoing life of the Church:

The Second Vatican Ecumenical Council in its deliberations and decrees assigned a singular importance to the liturgical rites, the ecclesiastical traditions, and the discipline of Christian life proper to those particular Churches, especially of the East, which are distinguished by their venerable antiquity, manifesting in various ways the tradition received through the Fathers from the Apostles (LA §4).

Indeed, the Roman Rite is a "precious example and instrument of true inculturation" (§5) in its ability to assimilate the genius of various peoples, especially in its orations. Yet some translations "have impeded the progress of the inculturation that actually should have taken place" (§6) – hence the need for the document.

Note the strong sense of the Roman tradition; but also, a sense for that which has been learned ("in the light of the maturing of experience").

In fact, it seems necessary to consider anew the true notion of liturgical translation in order that the translations of the Sacred Liturgy into the vernacular languages may stand secure as the authentic voice of the Church of God.[2] This Instruction therefore envisions and seeks to prepare for a new era of liturgical renewal, which is consonant with the qualities and the traditions of the particular Churches, but which safeguards also the faith and the unity of the whole Church of God (§7).

In *Comme le prévoit*, the world largely sets the standards for the Church; in *Liturgiam Authenticam*, the Church has its own tradition, it represents its own culture, and can and should have an effect on the world. In *Comme le prévoit*, Heraclitean *panta rhei* ("all is change") rules: one has the impression that all is changing, all the time. In *Liturgiam authenticam*, there is resistance to "frequent change" (§27) – to change for its own sake.

Impressive is the insistence in *Liturgiam Authenticam* that there be adaptability, flexibility in the worship life of the Church, but firmly within the context of her tradition.

Ideology Versus the Sacred

Perhaps not surprisingly, the 1960s saw both a great flowering of technological prowess and a romantic reaction to it. It was the great age of "experts" in all aspects of life. In *Comme le prévoit*, we see reliance on this very clearly. Though also wanting experts, *Liturgiam Authenticam* calls for "bishops who are expert" (§70) and explicitly calls for "a truly common effort rather than of any single person or of a small group of persons" – and again it is "the bishops" who are singled out as primarily responsible (§72).

Comme le prévoit had addressed itself primarily to the experts, while *Liturgiam Authenticam*, though acknowledging the need for experts, addresses itself to the bishops as the primary teachers. It allows that:

> The translation of liturgical texts requires not only a rare degree of expertise, but also a spirit of prayer and trust in the divine assistance granted not only to the translators, but to the Church herself, throughout the whole process leading to the definitive approbation of the texts (§75).

In effect, if this document is a blow to technocrats, to abstract language, and to academic manuals, I believe it aims to be a liberation of artists:

> To be avoided on this account are expressions characteristic of commercial publicity, political or ideological programs, passing fashions, and those which are subject to regional variations or ambiguities in meaning. Academic style manuals or similar works, since they sometimes give way to such tendencies, are not to be considered standards for liturgical translation. On the other hand, works that are commonly considered "classics" in a given vernacular language may prove useful in providing a suitable standard for its vocabulary and usage (§32).

> Modes of speech by which heavenly realities and actions are depicted in human form, or designated by means of limited, concrete terminology – as happens quite frequently in biblical language (i.e., anthropomorphisms) – often maintain their full force only if translated somewhat literally, as in the case of words in the *Nova Vulgata Editio* such as *ambulare, brachium, digitus, manus,* or *vultus [Dei]*, as well as *caro, cornu, os, semen,* and *visitare*. Thus it is best that such terms not be explained or interpreted by more abstract or general vernacular expressions. As regards certain terms, such as those translated in the *Nova Vulgata*

as *anima* and *spiritus*, the principles mentioned in above nn. 40–41 should be observed. Therefore, one should avoid replacing these terms by a personal pronoun or a more abstract term, except when this is strictly necessary in a given case. It should be borne in mind that a literal translation of terms which may initially sound odd in a vernacular language may for this very reason provoke inquisitiveness in the hearer and provide an occasion for catechesis (§43).

Liturgiam Authenticam stresses catechesis on the given (classical) form: it insists on respecting form. Paul Ricoeur has written that "the symbol invites thought"[3] – invites thought in a way that keeps symbols intact, so that they may continue to be fruitful sources of thought. The technocratic mind, on the other hand, tries to "reduce symbol to concept,"[4] and it is precisely this reductionism that translations have been effecting for thirty years. After the romantic excesses of the 1960s, some return to classical form was needed, and this document represents that return.

If indeed, in the liturgical texts, words or expressions are sometimes employed which differ somewhat from usual and everyday speech, it is often enough by virtue of this very fact that the texts become truly memorable and capable of expressing heavenly realities. Indeed, it will be seen that the observance of the principles set forth in this Instruction will contribute to the gradual development, in each vernacular, of a sacred style that will come to be recognized as proper to liturgical language. Thus it may happen that a certain manner of speech which has come to be considered somewhat obsolete in daily usage may continue to be maintained in the liturgical context. In translating biblical passages where seemingly inelegant words or expressions are used, a hasty tendency to sanitize this characteristic is likewise to be avoided. These principles, in fact, should free the Liturgy from the necessity of frequent revisions when modes of expression may have passed out of popular usage (§27).

Some other elements are worth noting.

The insistence on consistency in theological vocabulary is meant to resist a spirit of confusion:

> In order that the faithful may be able to commit to memory at least the more important texts of the Sacred Scriptures and be formed by them even in their private prayer, it is of the greatest importance that the translation of

the Sacred Scriptures intended for liturgical use be characterized by a certain uniformity and stability, such that in every territory there should exist only one approved translation, which will be employed in all parts of the various liturgical books. This stability is especially to be desired in the translation of the Sacred Books of more frequent use, such as the Psalter, which is the fundamental prayer book of the Christian people[5] (§36, cf. §41).

There is a welcome encouragement to produce dignified looking books for use by the laity – a turn away from "Missalettes."

The books from which the liturgical texts are recited in the vernacular with or on behalf of the people should be marked by such a dignity that the exterior appearance of the book itself will lead the faithful to a greater reverence for the word of God and for sacred realities.[6] Thus it is necessary as soon as possible to move beyond the temporary phase characterized by leaflets or fascicles, wherever these exist (§120).

Political manipulation – that is, "experiments," which are merely ways of introducing something that will later be un-removable – is opposed by the principle that "it is not permissible to publish, for the use of celebrants or for the general public, any liturgical texts that have been translated or recently composed, as long as the *recognitio* is lacking" (§80).

The practice of seeking the *recognitio* from the Apostolic See for all translations of liturgical books[7] accords the necessary assurance of the authenticity of the translation and its correspondence with the original texts. This practice both expresses and effects a bond of communion between the successor of blessed Peter and his brothers in the Episcopate. Furthermore, this *recognitio* is not a mere formality, but is rather an exercise of the power of governance, which is absolutely necessary (§80).

It has been said that the "Rhine Flowed into the Tiber" in the 1960s: that a Western Europe that had shown its spiritual bankruptcy, and was dazed by the Bauhaus in architecture, was left further drained by the War – and yet it somehow seemed to dominate the Council. It is argued that scientific triumphalism, which should have been checked by the events of the war, experienced a certain victory in the Church. We can see something of this in *Comme le prévoit*, where its authors' unquestioning faith in a certain vision of democracy that is, mere majority rule, the search for the lowest common denominator evidently replaced any regard for quality; and so, to the authors of *Comme le prévoit*, poetry is unacceptable, or, if poetry there must be, it must be "common poetry" (CLP §15).

The 1960s were the age of the New Left in France, the thirst for a vision in the wasteland, the reaching out to Marxist models. Thus emerged a strange mix of technocracy and romantic rebellion, two spirits that feed on each other, without creating an integrated vision. In the rules for translation of *Comme le prévoit*, we see technocratic man attempting to conceptualize that which might best be left suggestive – and imaginatively fruitful – to "reduce symbol to concept."

In *Comme le prévoit*, language is a vehicle for conveying abstract ideas: one has the impression of excessive reverence for "modern concepts" (CLP §33). In *Liturgiam Authenticam*, the word itself is respected: the beauty of language, a language that can be memorized, because it is "truly memorable and capable of expressing heavenly realities" (LA §27; cf. 48, 64). Language is allowed to have symbolic depths and overtones that are lost if human speech is merely a tool to convey concepts.

The existentialist philosopher, Martin Heidegger, saw his German culture as the one alternative to the mass barbarisms of Soviet Bolshevism and American consumerism. Tragically, a paganized Germany succumbed to the Nazi vision and the perversion and destruction of European Christian civilization within its empire. The present Holy Father, a student of literature and drama, and a creative artist himself, is a man of the word, and he has brought to light a dimension to the Church that was ignored at the time *Comme le prévoit* was written. Perhaps *Liturgiam Authenticam* could only have been written after the collapse of the Marxist alternative, and a growing disenchantment with what Hans Urs von Balthasar called the *"anima technica vacua."*[8] Hence, the call to a return to a more ancient tradition.

Although *Liturgiam Authenticam* affirms the benefits of modern scholarship and technical prowess, it rejects the tyranny of experts, and allows the spirit of art, of poetry, of excellence and quality to reclaim their place. The technocratic bias of the twentieth century is corrected: beauty re-claims her place in religious language. Indeed, language itself can be healed: feminine pronouns are allowed to return along with the masculine, as befits an incarnate religion, a hopeful sign if it means greater fidelity to Scripture and the Mind that created it.

Though respected and indeed essential to the work of translation, academic meritocracy is invited to yield pride of place to the hierarchal principle embodied in the Church's episcopal leadership.

Like her chief shepherd, with *Liturgiam Authenticam*, the Catholic Church speaks with a new and fearless confidence in the ruins of the modern West, summoning us to the task of weaving the best of contemporary culture into the continuing life of the tradition. The deep resonance that this document seems to accord with the spirit of the Church being reborn among us should be cause for a real if sober optimism. *Benedicamus Domino!*

Note: In addition to being delivered at the FCS Omaha convention, this paper also appeared in the November, 2001, issue of the *Adoremus Bulletin*. I am especially indebted to Dr. Stephen Beall and the members of the Marquette *Communio* Discussion Group for many of the insights here.

Father Raymond T. Gawronski, S.J., is an Assistant Professor of Theology at Marquette University in Milwaukee. He is also an aggregate member of Mount Tabor Byzantine Catholic Monastery in Redwood Valley, California. See the note following his Regular Conference Session talk on "The Beauty of the Cross: The Theological Aesthetics of Hans Urs von Balthasar" earlier in this volume for further biographical information.

Notes

1   We live in an age that believes in matter and not in spirit, in quantity and not in quality, in feelings but not in form. I am indebted to Huston Smith and through him the school of thought around René Guenon for a renewed sense of reverence for tradition.

2   Cf. Pope Paul VI, Address to translators of liturgical texts into vernacular languages, November 10, 1965: AAS 57 (1965) 968.

3   *The Philosophy of Paul Ricoeur*, Ed., Charles E. Regan and David Stewart (Boston: Beacon Press, 1978), p. 46.

4   I am indebted to Marquette graduate student Christopher Dorn for this phrase and insight.

5   Cf. Pope Paul VI, Apost. Const. Laudis canticum, November 1, 1970. N. 8: AAS 63 (1971),532–533; Officium Divinum, Liturgia Horarum iuxta Ritum romanum, editio typica altera 1985: Instituto Generalis de Liturgia

Horarum, n. 100; Pope John Paul II, Apost. Letter Vicesimus quintus annus, n. 8: AAS 81 (1989) 904–905.

6 Cf. Second Vatican Council, Const. Sacrosanctum Concilium, n. 122; S. Congr. Of Rites, Instr. Inter Oecumenici, n. 40 e: AAS 56 (1964) 886.

7 Cf. Second Vatican Council, Const. Sacrosanctum Concilium, n. 36; S. Congr. of Rites, Instr. Inter Oecumenici, nn. 20–21, 31: AAS (1964) 882, 884; Code of Canon Law, can. 838.

8 Hans Urs von Balthasar, *Epilog* (Einsiedeln: Johannes Verlag, 1987), p. 8.

FELLOWSHIP OF CATHOLIC SCHOLARS

Membership Information
http://www4.DESALES.edu/-philtheo/FCS/

Statement of Purpose

We, Catholic Scholars in various disciplines, join in fellowship in order to serve Jesus Christ better, by helping one another in our work and by putting our abilities more fully at the service of the Catholic faith.

We wish to form a Fellowship of Catholic Scholars who see their intellectual work as expressing the service they owe to God. To Him we give thanks for our Catholic faith and for every opportunity He gives us to serve that faith.

We wish to form a Fellowship of Catholic Scholars open to the work of the Holy Spirit within the Church. Thus we wholeheartedly accept and support the renewal of the Church of Christ undertaken by Pope John XXIII, shaped by Vatican Council II, and carried on by succeeding popes.

We accept as the rule of our life and the thought the entire faith of the Catholic Church. This we see not merely in solemn definitions but in the ordinary teaching of the pope and the bishops in union with him, and also embodied in those modes of worship and ways of Christian life, of the present as of the past, which have been in harmony with the teaching of St. Peter's successors in the See of Rome.

To contribute to this sacred work, our Fellowship will strive to:

- Come to know and welcome all who share our purpose;
- Make known to one another our various competencies and interests;
- Share our abilities with one another unstintingly in our efforts directed to our common purpose;
- Cooperate in clarifying the challenges which must be met;
- Help one another to evaluate critically the variety of responses which are proposed to these challenges;

· Communicate our suggestions and evaluations to members of the Church who might find them helpful;
· Respond to requests to help the Church in her task of guarding the faith as inviolable and defending it with fidelity;
· Help one another to work through, in scholarly and prayerful fashion and without public dissent, any problem which may arise from magisterial teaching.

With the grace of God for which we pray, we hope to assist the whole Church to understand her own identity more clearly, to proclaim the joyous gospel of Jesus more confidently, and to carry out its redemptive to all humankind more effectively.

To apply for membership, contact:

Rev. Thomas F. Dailey, O.S.F.S.
FCS President
DeSales University
2755 Station Avenue
Center Valley, PA 18034–9568
TEL: (610) 282–1100, Ext. 1464
E–mail: THOMAS.DAILEY@DESALES.EDU

Member Benefits

Fellowship of Catholic Scholars Quarterly – All members receive four issues annually. This approximately 50-page publication includes:

President's Page
Scholarly articles
Important Documentation
Bulletin Board (news)
Book Reviews
Occasional Fellowship symposia

National Conventions – All members are invited to attend this annual gathering, held in various cities where, by custom, the local ordinary greets and typically celebrates Mass for the members of the Fellowship. The typical convention program includes:

Daily Mass
Keynote Address

At least six scholarly Sessions

Banquet and Awards

Membership business meeting and occasional substantive meetings on subjects of current interest to the Fellowship's membership

Current members receive a copy of the published *Proceedings*, containing the texts of the speeches of each national convention, with other material of interest sometimes included.

National Awards – The Fellowship grants the following awards, usually presented during the annual convention.

The Cardinal Wright Award – given *annually* to a Catholic adjudged to have done an outstanding service for the Church in the tradition of the late Cardinal John J. Wright, Bishop of Pittsburgh and later Prefect of the Congregation for the Clergy in Rome. The recipients of this Award have been:

1979 – Rev. Msgr. George A. Kelly

1980 – Dr. William E. May

1981 – Dr. James Hitchcock

1982 – Dr. Germain Grisez

1983 – Rev. John Connery, S.J.

1984 – Rev. John A. Hardon, S.J.

1985 – Dr. Herbert Ratner

1986 – Dr. Joseph P. Scottino

1987 – Rev. Joseph Farraher, S.J., & Rev. Joseph Fessio, S.J.

1988 – Rev. John Harvey, O.S.F.S.

1989 – Dr. John Finnis

1990 – Rev. Ronald Lawler, O.F.M. Cap.

1991 – Rev. Francis Canavan, S.J.

1992 – Rev. Donald J. Keefe, S.J.

1993 – Dr. Janet E. Smith

1994 – Dr. Jude P. Dougherty

1995 – Rev. Msgr. William B. Smith

1996 – Dr. Ralph McInerny

1997 – Rev. James V. Schall, S.J.

1998 – Rev. Msgr. Michael J. Wrenn & Mr. Kenneth D. Whitehead

1999 – Dr. Robert P. George

2000 – Dr. Mary Ann Glendon

2001 – Thomas W. Hilgers, M.D.

The Cardinal O'Boyle Award – This award is given *occasionally* to individuals who actions demonstrate a courage and witness in favor of the Catholic faith similar to that exhibited by the late Cardinal Patrick A. O'Boyle, Archbishop of Washington, in the face of the pressures of our contemporary society which tend to undermine the faith. The recipients of this award have been:

1988 – Rev. John C. Ford, S.J.
1991 – Mother Angelica, P.C.P.A., EWTN
1995 – John and Sheila Kippley, Couple to Couple League
1997 – Rep. Henry J. Hyde (R.-IL)